The Franchise Formula

2nd Edition

Step By Step Online Marketing Success for Franchisors and Franchisees

Michael J. Meyer

The Franchise Formula
2nd Edition

Step By Step Online Marketing Success for Franchisors and Franchisees

Copyright © 2014 by Michael J. Meyer

ISBN: 978-1500882105

Acknowledgments

A book like this is not written by one person alone. There are many people who helped in ways both subtle and elaborate.

I would like to thank those franchisees who answered my detailed questions as well as the franchisors who shared their valuable insights.

I also wish to thank the team at NetSearch Direct for their hard work. Their talent and dedication never cease to amaze me.

And, of course, **thank you** for taking the time to read the solutions offered within this book. As always, please feel free to reach me at:

804-228-4400
mikem@netsearchdirect.com

I would love to hear from you.

Credits

Written by Michael J. Meyer

Edited by Caroline Hall, Natalie Iannello, and Kriti Gangal

Disclaimer

This book is presented solely for educational and entertainment purposes. The author and publisher are not offering it as legal, accounting, or other professional services advice. While best efforts have been used in preparing this book, the author and publisher make no representations or warranties of any kind and assume no liabilities of any kind with respect to the accuracy or completeness of the contents and specifically disclaim any implied warranties of merchantability or fitness of use for a particular purpose. Neither the author nor the publisher shall be held liable or

Conventions Used

The goal of this book is to provide clear and simple solutions to some of the most common and trying online marketing challenges faced by franchisors and franchisees. That said; we didn't mess around with little cartoon icons and big space-wasting images.

Aside from the regular **section headings** and **sub-headings** you expect to see, you will find only a few simple conventions used in this book. Their sole purpose is to bring something noteworthy to your attention. Here they are:

Call Outs: "These quotes are nice and big and just serve as reinforcement to an important point." (Note: Not all call outs are quotes.)

Word Opp:

This is an inline glossary of sorts to introduce you to terms that might be new to you, or have multiple meanings. Word Opps can quickly be spotted by their font and format as shown here.

Examples: Once in a while we need to show a PPC ad example to explain a point quickly and accurately. These are obvious, but we have also altered the shade of the text to make them stand out just a bit more.

That's it. Let's get going!

A Note from the Author

Welcome to the second edition of The Franchise Formula. A great deal has changed in the world of online marketing since this book's first release in 2012. Even as this book goes to press, Google very recently released its Pigeon algorithm update and it's taking the local search community by storm. But that's just one change of many. Throughout this book you will discover dozens of subtle and not so subtle changes to the WWW landscape.

For me, writing this update was even more exciting because so many of the aforementioned changes had a pronounced effect on franchises business; a subject near and dear to my heart as you will soon see...

I grew up as the son of a small business owner, a franchisee. I saw my father leave his (from my teenage perspective) safe, cushy job with the Virginia Department of Agriculture to fulfill his dream of going into business for himself…as a janitor. Please understand that I have a lot of respect for those in the cleaning industry. Little did I know that I was about to learn a whole lot about cleaning – cleaning toilets, cleaning carpets, walls and ceilings, cleaning up after fires and floods.

However, as sophomore in high school my perspective was, shall we say, self-centered and immature. How could my Dad leave his safe, cushy, state job to clean buildings? There was this thing called "college" looming in the not too distant future and I had heard it was kind of expensive. How the heck was that going to happen?

As you can imagine my life was about to change, in more ways than I could envision. First and foremost I was about to learn the true meaning of a family business. Since I was a member of the family, I now was part of the business and expected to work, and work and work…in this business. Consumption of food is on just about every teenage boy's "top ten" list, and if I wanted to eat… Well you get the idea.

But there was something else that this new business was about to teach me. My dad had bought a franchise, specifically a janitorial franchise from ServiceMaster, Inc. Back in 1975, the franchise industry was relatively young. Up until that point in my life I probably didn't even know what a franchise was – and/or didn't really care. However, my Dad's new business, specifically a franchise business, would without a doubt have an indelible effect on my career path many years later.

So let's fast-forward a few decades. The apple didn't fall far from the tree. Although I didn't end up going into the family business, I did become a franchisee. I will never forget that day. I had arrived. I now had something I could call my own. I was in charge - no one to tell me what to do or how to do it. All those years when I said to myself, "Well if I was the owner, I would do it this way," or, "We could be much more profitable if we just did this" were now in the past. It was a new era, with a new sheriff in town…me. Well almost. I soon learned that as a franchisee I actually had a "partner" in my business – the franchisor.

This was both good, and at times, not so good. Believe it or not, sometimes the franchisor didn't always see things the way I did. As an independent business owner I had my own ideas, as did other franchisees and my franchisor – and a whole new world of franchising was about to teach me many, many lessons.

These, combined with what I have learned in the Search Engine Marketing industry are the basis for this book. Owning a franchise has taught me more about business than I ever learned in school. It would never have happened if my Dad hadn't become a janitor...and a franchisee. Thanks Dad.

Introduction

My name is Mike Meyer. I am the president and CEO of NetSearch Direct, a Richmond, Virginia based online marketing company. But that's not important. What is important is how my experience, with helping franchisors and franchisees increase sales and profits, can benefit YOU.

My team and I have been working within the franchise industry for more than seven years. And of our six-hundred-plus clients, a full third of them are franchisees or franchisors. That's more than two hundred franchisee business owners and franchisors that have experienced a major win through our services. And this is to say nothing of the other small and large businesses of nearly every type imaginable. I mention that not to boast (okay, maybe just a little) but rather to ensure you the tactics and techniques you are about to read really work. And work well.

But will they work for you? That's the same question everyone who contacts me has in mind. So let's dig in and find out. While I am not at liberty to disclose company names (a benefit all who use our services enjoy) I can name industries and exact specialties.

Following is a partial list, set in no particular order. Please keep in mind that some categories have more than twenty individual clients while others might have just one or two...

- ✓ **Professional:** Accountants, Attorneys, Consultants, Insurance Agencies, etc.
- ✓ **Health Care:** General, Specialty, Dental, and Rehabilitation
- ✓ **Wellness:** Massage, Therapy (non-medical), Consultants, Retirement, etc.
- ✓ **Beauty:** Facial Techs, Hair Salons, Nail Salons, Body Wrap Spas - You name it

- ✓ **Fitness:** Aerobic Studios, Various Gyms, Fitness Consultants, etc.
- ✓ **Dining:** Formal, Fast Food, Catering, Box Lunches, and everything in-between
- ✓ **Entertainment:** Clubs, Sporting Events, Event Management, etc.
- ✓ **Automotive:** Car Window Tinting, Auto Glass Replacement, Detailing, etc.
- ✓ **Transportation:** Limousines to Big Rig Carriers and Big Box Movers/Storage
- ✓ **Home Improvement Interior:** Plumbers, Electricians, HVAC, Carpenters, Stone Specialists, Window Tint Specialists
- ✓ **Home Improvement Exterior:** Painters, Replacement Window Specialists, Glass Replacement Specialists, Landscapers, etc.
- ✓ **Maintenance:** Carpet Cleaners, Home and Office Janitorial, Tile and Grout Experts, Duct Cleaners, Disaster Recovery Specialists, and more
- ✓ **Retail Offerings:** Office Products, Jewelry, Clothing, Sporting Goods, etc.

✓ **Franchising:** Yes, we even work with a major franchising company that helps interested entrepreneurs get in with the optimal franchise to meet their needs.

Again, this is just a partial list to demonstrate the breadth of experience and how the solutions outlined in these pages can help you succeed, whether you are a franchisor or franchisee - or even still deciding if you want to buy in to a franchise.

When supplied with the proper information, your earning potential is almost unlimited. Now it's time to put it to work for you.

Note to Returning Readers:
*If you read the first edition of this book you might want to jump to Page 20 – **Part Zero: Since Last We Met.** It contains 37 pages of new material that also guides you through many of the updates to other new material within the book.*

Table of Contents

2014 Update

Although briefly mentioned in both the Author's Note section and Introduction, a great deal has happened with online marketing since this book's first release 2 ½ years ago.

Much of the information in this book is brand new while some of the "new" concepts we'll be covering have been around for years – but are just now becoming main-stream and/or making a large impact on the landscape. Videos, for example have been around forever – but custom developed *explainer videos* are sweeping the world, one viral share at a time.

If you'd like to jump to the latest and greatest, go ahead over to page 20 – Part Zero: When Last We Met. If you never read the first edition of this book, you may want to start at the beginning,

Enjoy.

The Tug of War

Over the past five years we have worked with more than one hundred fifty franchisors and franchisees, making it easy for their potential customers to find them online through search engine optimization (SEO), pay-per-click advertising (PPC) and Social Media (Social). Through the years we have heard the same thing nearly every time - from both groups...

"It's like a tug of war."

I'm sure you know exactly what they mean. The franchisor has to do what they think is right, which means a lot of restrictions, and the franchisee needs to make a profit while working within approved (and typically somewhat stringent) guidelines.

What if I told you that this online marketing tug of war could be a win for everybody?

1

Prepare to be excited, because it really can! After all, franchisors and franchisees both want the same thing: success of the brand and "store" location.

Keep in mind; the wants and needs of both groups are what most would consider the bare essentials.

Although every organization varies with its exact wants and needs, it's usually safe to assume the following:

Franchisors want...

- ✓ to control the message
- ✓ to protect the brand
- ✓ to manage the web presence
- ✓ to appeal to multiple GEO markets (parts of the state, country or even world)
- ✓ to market to both consumers and potential franchisees

In comparison, franchisees want...

- ✓ to control their own offers
- ✓ marketing and advertising flexibility
- ✓ to control their own web presence
- ✓ to show up locally on Google, Yahoo and Bing
- ✓ to beat the local competition and maximize profit

There's more of course, but these are the big ticket items just about everyone in the industry can agree upon.

Now get ready for the really great news. This book addresses ALL of the above with quick and easy solutions that will leave everyone smiling and nobody feeling left out.

Getting To Know You

If you ever find yourself saying, "Why are they being so unreasonable?" or, "What's the big deal?" don't skip this section. Sometimes we all lose sight of the fact that it's not "us against them" and, in fact, we are all on the same team.

With that in mind, this book is NOT divided into sections for franchisors and franchisees, but rather it has been carefully segmented into common goals that demonstrate how each party can attain what they want and make every potential challenge a "win-win".

Before we dive in to the thick of it, a few notes on what you can expect. This is just a two minute time investment to make sure this book is right for you before you spend any additional time.

What to Expect

I'll keep this short because your time is valuable. You can expect this book to be...

Concise: Concise is often used as another word for short, but it means more. Concise is also complete. Although this book is short on words, it is big on meaning. There's no fluff and filler here.

A quick read: This book will likely take less than two hours to read and <u>really understand</u>. It's all about fast, easy-to-implement solutions to improve your marketing, thus earnings, as quickly as possible.

Easy to understand: Only an idiot would write a book to help you and then fill it with big complex theories and formulas with the hope of impressing you. I promise, if you read this book through, you will "get it".

Full of potential options: You will see solutions that will work for your situation but, also, possibly some that will not. This is important. Every single solution offered in this book has worked in the franchise world - but one size does not fit all. Some organizations have very good reasons for not implementing a seemingly great idea. That's okay. The goal is to get as many wins as possible, not to undermine the core concepts of your organization or your own business.

That's about it. Let's get going.

Online Marketing Defined

Let's spend a minute wrapping a definition around "online marketing". In short, we can define it as any marketing effort conducted via the Internet. That's simple enough. Let's take it a step further and define "interactive marketing", which is almost always lumped into the same definition but should not be. For something to be "interactive" it must invite or invoke an action from a participant. For example, when a potential customer performs a search on Google (note the interaction) and sees your listing come up, they must click that listing to go to your page (even more interaction). That's classified as "interactive" because they have interacted with the search engine to reach their desired goal.

I don't want to get too technical here. I just want you to know the difference so some slick-talking marketer never has the upper-hand in negotiations. Knowing their language, and being able to "call BS", is one of the best negotiating skills you can have.

That said; let's quickly define three types of online marketing: SEO, PPC and Social...

SEO - *Short for Search Engine Optimization*, SEO is actually a slightly misleading name. You are not optimizing the search engine but rather, you are making your website more easily found on the search engines when somebody searches for particular keywords. If you've ever done a search on Google, Bing, or another search engine, you know that there are typically thousands or even millions of search results for just about any word or phrase. Proper SEO gets your website closer to the top of that list rather than somewhere down near the bottom where nobody is likely to see it.

That last part is important, so remember...

"Proper SEO gets your website closer to the top of a list of search results rather than somewhere down near the bottom where nobody is likely to see it."

The main advantage to SEO is that you are not paying for each visit but rather for organic (natural) optimization that can bring in leads for a fraction of the cost of paid advertising programs. But that tells only a tiny bit of the story. See **Desperately Seeking You** after this section for the really amazing part.

PPC - An acronym for *Pay-Per-Click*, PPC is just like it sounds. You can bid (auction style) to have your search engine listing come up when a particular keyword is searched. The potential visitor clicks on your listing if it appeals to their needs, at which time you pay an amount based on your bid.

The listings show in a special "Ads" or "Advertisement" section of the search engine results page, usually at the top and/or the right-hand side of the page.

Social - *Social Media* is a broad category that encompasses sites like Facebook, Twitter and LinkedIn, which are all business or casual networking platforms that allow people to quickly share the latest events in their lives or businesses. Most people use these resources to reconnect with or stay in touch with old friends as well as to meet new acquaintances with similar interests, from the comfort of their computer, tablet or smart-phone.

Now that we've covered the basics, we can take a few minutes and explore the main benefits of each...

Desperately Seeking... You!

When someone reaches your web page through SEO or Pay-Per-Click, it is because THEY searched for YOU. You have not tried to sell them anything yet. They walked right into your door and said, without you having to ask, "I am looking for XYZ and Google told me I could find it here."

Do you have any idea how incredibly powerful that is? They want what you have to offer - and they know it.

Instant Gratification

Although it can be costly if not carefully monitored, PPC provides nearly instant results, unlike SEO that takes time to build organically. Instant gratification is its biggest feature.

"PPC provides nearly instant results."

Here's a little inside tip - you can use PPC to get quick results for a couple months while your SEO is ramping up.

This option provides the best of both worlds for anyone who wants quick leads as well as lower-cost sustainable lead and sales generation.

Going Viral

Social Media's biggest advantage is its "viral" capabilities. If you grew up in the 80's you might remember the **_Faberge Organic Shampoo_** ™ commercial with Heather Locklear. If not, I'll walk you through:

Her face is framed to take up the full screen and she says, "I told two friends, and they told two friends, and so on, and so on..." Then you see the screen quickly fill up with hundreds of Heathers, showing the power of word of mouth advertising.

Social Media is like that, but more accurately, "I told ten friends, and they told ten friends, and so on...", IF it's done properly.

Do You Have Fans?

It's important to note that although all businesses could potentially benefit from social media marketing, some do better than others because their industry is already very "fan based".

Working with the first thing that comes to mind when you think of "fans", anything in the entertainment arena generally has enormous potential in social media. In fact, some garage bands have gone gold just from Facebook and Twitter exposure. And the impact of YouTube goes without saying.

This is not to say that a plumbing company could not benefit from social. The above is merely a note to help set expectations that a plumbing company is not likely to attract as many followers as a restaurant that regularly posts specials and new menu items. Think of it like this... Most people have a favorite restaurant, coffee shop, night spot, etc. Fewer people have a favorite plumber, electrician, or windshield replacement company.

The easiest way to summarize is simply to say that the more something is frequented, the more likely it is to attract followers. This usually falls into the areas considered prime for disposable income.

But don't get me wrong. Beyond all other things, social media sites like Facebook are in themselves entertainment spots - gathering places for people with similar interests or relationships. That said, these can be great places to get the word out for ANY business.

Does Your Product Warrant Research?

Even if some service industries or particular products may not attract a lot of fans, that's okay. In fact, thanks to YouTube, it's no problem at all. Having a YouTube Channel is like having your own special soapbox where you can display your wares and your services - typically through short instructional videos or video tours of products.

We have yet to see an industry or franchise that is not a good fit for YouTube.

Challenges Are Opportunities

Years of experience and the opportunity to work with more than one hundred fifty franchisors and franchisees have taught us more than we ever dreamed possible about the intricacies of online marketing for franchises. As you might already know, search engine optimization and pay-per-click advertising (SEO and PPC) for franchises is considerably different than for independent businesses. So is Social Media for that matter. You encounter all of the regular challenges with at least five more thrown into the mix. It's those five challenges (unique and often detrimental to the franchise world) that we will focus on in this short book.

Before I go on however, let me say that challenges are not bad. In fact, like so many difficult things we experience, once a challenge has been overcome it actually puts us in a better position to tackle the next. Or, ideally, if no other challenge immediately presents itself we can overcome the competition like never before. And that's exactly how it is for SEO, PPC and Social. Once you have come to an agreement on how to handle a "tug of war" issue, the rest falls into place - seemingly at Mach speed (at least as compared to what you are used to).

So don't dread the challenges. Over the course of this book you will learn how to overcome each easily as it comes up, and be much stronger - and a great deal more successful - for the effort.

Part Zero: Since Last We Met

To make things easier for anyone looking for the latest updates to this book, I've included this quick little section called Part Zero.

Although there have been updates made throughout the whole of this book, to bring samples up to date, every effort has been made to keep the information as close to the original as possible. This is so you will not need to re-read sections you may already be familiar with from the original 2012 edition.

Here you find eight new sections falling under four major categories, as follow…

SEO:
- ✓ *SEO Update 2014*
- ✓ *Beyond Algorithm Updates*
- ✓ *Don't Be Fooled by Faux SEO*
- ✓ *Faux SEO - Buyer Beware*

Google+, Maps and Local Listings:
- ✓ *Getting Local*

Mobile Web & SEO:
- ✓ Think Local; Act Mobile

PPC:
- ✓ *PPC Update 2014*

Chat:
- ✓ *Worth Chatting About*

Video:
- ✓ *Video Made the Internet Star*
- ✓ *Video Types*
- ✓ *Video Styles*

The idea here is to make this as convenient as possible for you with all of the new stuff in one place and the technical samples updated throughout. Enjoy!

SEO Update 2014

A lot has changed with SEO since the first edition of this book was published in 2012. In addition to the obvious Panda and Penguin Google algorithm updates, there have been a handful that affected more sites than others...

DMCA Penalty: August 2012

Google began penalizing sites guilty of repeated copyright violations. This was most likely due to an excessive number of DMCA takedown requests.

DMCA refers to the 1998 Digital Millennium Copyright Act. This act is a part of the Online Copyright Infringement Liability Limitation Act (OCILLA) that has flooded Google with requests to remove webpages in violation from their index.

65 Pack: October 2012

There were a handful of major updates as part of this "65 Pack". The biggest affecting local franchisee business had to do with 1.) how Google determines page quality, 2.) how the relevancy of local results are determined and 3.) their updated autocomplete feature, which helps shape how people search. Following are excerpts from Google's release explaining the updates…

"**LTS**. [project "*Other Ranking Components*"] We improved our web ranking to determine what pages are relevant for queries containing locations."

"[project "*Page Quality*"] This launch helped you find more high-quality content from trusted sources."

"**nearby**. [project "*User Context*"] We improved the precision and coverage of our system to help you find more relevant local web results. Now we're better able to identify web results that are local to the user, and rank them appropriately."

"[project "*User Context*"] We made improvements to show more relevant local results."

"**essence**. [project "*Autocomplete*"] This change introduced entity predictions in autocomplete. Now Google will predict not just the string of text you might be looking for, but the actual real-world thing. Clarifying text will appear in the drop-down box to help you disambiguate your search."

"[project "*Autocomplete*"] This change tweaked the display of real-world entities in autocomplete to reduce repetitiveness. With this change, we don't show the entity name (displayed to the right of the dash) when it's fully contained in the query."

"**TSSPC**. [project "*Spelling*"] This change used spelling algorithms to improve the relevance of long-tail autocomplete predictions."

Above the Fold *(aka "Page Layout 2" and "Top Heavy"):* **October 2012**

This update penalized pages with too many ads showing above the fold of a webpage (the immediately visible portion of the screen - before you have to scroll). While many franchise websites were not affected by this update, due to the back-end structure of the design that placed most text below the fold, plenty were.

Please Note: There was another update in February 2014, to be aware of.

Penguin 2.0: May 2013

The judge, jury and executioner of Web-spam, Penguin came out with a more targeted agenda in May 2013. As Matt Cutts, of Google fame, promised – Penguin 2.0 went deeper and sniffed out more bad links and link schemes.

In general this should not be any more or less relevant to franchise websites, however we at NetSearch Direct found that the link-spam actions of a handful of franchisee sites can adversely affect the entire franchisor network of sites. Simply put; a few bad apples really can ruin the bunch.

Hummingbird: August 2013

This is the really BIG change. Hummingbird was not just an algorithm change but a rebuild in how Google performs search. Switching from the traditional Boolean search model of simply combing words without understanding intent, Hummingbird uses something called semantic search. In short, semantic search is more about the intent of the search than simply the words used to perform the search.

As defined by Wikipedia:

"Semantic search seeks to improve search accuracy by understanding searcher intent and the contextual meaning of terms as they appear in the searchable dataspace, whether on the Web or within a closed system, to generate more relevant results."

Panda 4.0: May 2014

Panda is all about preventing pages with poor or "thin" content from topping Google's SERPs (Search Engine Results Pages).

Although there have been plenty of updates since its initial 2011 release, Panda 4.0 is more like a new Panda than a simple algorithm refresh due to its comprehensive nature. This update sniffed out thin content with a whole new degree of scrutiny.

Pigeon: July 2014

The Google Pigeon algorithm update began rolling out on July 24, 2014 and by the 25th, millions of local business websites were wondering one of two things; "Why did I just disappear from page one?" and "How did I get to page one overnight?". The short answer is "proximity". Pigeon was Google's latest attempt to make local search even more local and it affected not only the regular SERPs but also the map listings (Google+).

Beyond Algorithm Updates

We focused a lot on algorithm updates for obvious reasons, but the changes to SEO go beyond simple dos and don'ts. The tremendous increase in mobile and tablet device use has changed the standards of web design in many regards.

However, even if Google is not "officially" giving preference to mobile-enable sites, we've seen enough unofficial results to say it's in your best interest to be as mobile-friendly as possible (aka use a responsive design). It's not like there have not been hints since late 2011 when Google released a new mobile user agent for Googlebot-Mobile smartphone (December 2011). Of course, with their stake in mobile, as the owners of DROID, this should come as no surprise.

In June 2012, at SMX Advanced during the iSEO panel, Google Webmaster Trends Analyst, Pierre Far, detailed Google's preferences on mobile web design and leaned strongly toward "responsive" design. Responsive Web design, or RWD, presents the same content for desktop, tablet and traditional mobile devices (smartphone). The technology uses cascading style sheets, or CSS, to present the content in the most appropriate format to match the device being used.

It will come to no surprise that, in late 2014, SEO on mobile sites is becoming more important than ever since most mobile search is geared toward finding local solutions.

All of this said; short of redesigning your site to be responsive you can still get plenty of mobile-friendly SEO bang for your buck with a few simple, low-cost methods. We'll cover that in a future section called **"Think Local; Act Mobile"**.

Don't Be Fooled by Faux SEO

Over the past couple years there has been a barrage of new so-called "SEO" services hitting the marketplace. I call this Faux SEO.

Why Faux SEO? Because the product being delivered is not search engine optimization but those selling it swear that is. If you want a comparison, consider this scenario…

You go to an open market where two vendors are selling, what appear to be, identical leather jackets. The vendor on the right has the jacket you like in genuine leather for $299. The vendor on the left has one that looks very similar for just $99, and it's even a bit shinier! He tells you it's genuine. He just forgot to mention that it's genuine pleather – not leather.

Excuse the play on words; but choose the right vendor.

I choose to believe that no company would intentionally mislead you about the services you are paying for, but it's a good idea to have them explain exactly what you will be getting. I don't mean an overall description or "broad strokes", but the actual quantifiable work and expected results.

So what is Faux SEO?

There are several variations out there in the world today. Here is the one that popped up the most throughout 2013 and '14:

Directory Listings Management

In of itself, Directory Listings Management is a valuable tool to have and can do good things for your business – but it is NOT true SEO. It's basically just adding your company

name, address, phone number, and other
business information into a bunch of directories such as Merchant Circle and different
online "Yellow Pages". This is done in the
attempt to attract referral visits from those
directories to your website and often with an
over-inflated estimate of backlink value.

If done properly, there's nothing wrong with
it, and it can even help your web presence by
reinforcing your NAP data (name, address,
and phone) across multiple parts of the Web.
The only thing that's wrong is calling it search
engine optimization.

You see, true ongoing SEO involves a lot
more than adding your business's name,
address, and phone data into an automated
tool that then distributes it to 200 directories
– and hoping it gets picked up (like so many
Directory Listings Management programs).
SEO, in fact, involves both on-site and off-

site factors to help steer your site to ranking success.

True SEO

Onsite practices include optimizing on-page content, carefully crafting Meta tags, building ideal Header tags, working with Alt tags, balancing keyword density, volume, proximity, and weight – as well as making sure everything is written for human eyes and can easily ace Google's natural text algorithm checks.

Offsite work includes building links (a very difficult art in itself), leveraging supporting websites, gaining both page and domain authority while accumulating citations and trust flow from diverse online mediums.

This takes A LOT of work; both during initial setup and ongoing work, month over month.

Faux SEO - Buyer Beware

Before we close on this topic, I would like to offer a few words to the wise.

Directory listing management can be valuable in of itself, but its greatest value presents itself as a compliment to true ongoing SEO. Why is it better with SEO?

First and foremost, directories fall out of favor with Google all of the time. Today's "hot backlinks" can easily become tomorrow's link spam that you end up paying an SEO professional to get rid of for you. I know because this is how we, at NetSearch Direct, get about 20% of our new customers.

Secondly and equally important, is the true ROI factor. There are some services that will knowingly or unknowingly misrepresent one or more time-tested methods for showing return on investment. For this discussion, we'll look at call tracking.

Call tracking is a great tool for any business owner who is not restricted by HIPAA or similar confidentiality regulations. In short, you place a call tracking script on your website that helps you track how people got to your site if they call you. This is usually very good. I swear by it because it lets our clients see if calls came in by organic visits, through paid clicks, by referral (such as an email link or site link) or if they simply typed the URL and got to the site directly.

Unfortunately, there are some people claiming to provide SEO, who simply use a script that counts all organic, direct and referral visits as "SEO". They do this by using a special "tracking number" in all of those directories they listed you with.

When questioned, they might argue "Well, we did post the script that sent your NAP data to 200 directories." While that might be true, why do they insist on tracking inbound leads as "organic" when they are actually referral? An even better question is why would they count direct visits as organic search driven?

Think about it. By tracking most or all leads as organic, they will get credit for every website visit from...

- ✓ Business cards your techs hand out
- ✓ Direct mail piece you send out
- ✓ Radio spot you run
- ✓ Television ads broadcast
- ✓ Email campaign click that you receive
- ✓ And even Word-of-Mouth advertising!

That's all YOUR hard work. Not only does it remove tremendously inflate "organic" leads, but it also eliminates any chance you have of knowing what other advertising works for you. Talk about a bad idea!

One more thing... Do yourself a favor and ask them about the accuracy of that Name, Address, and Phone data.

If they posted a phone number to 200 directories that is tied to THEIR call tracking system, and you ever leave their services, you may lose all of those future calls.

At the very least, ask if there is an option for you to take ownership of the call tracking number. It's not a perfect solution, but at least you can keep getting leads.

Google+, Maps, and Local Listings

Often referred to as *"Local Business Directory Listings"*, or LBDLs, most people simply call them the *maps sections* or *local listings*.

This is where people go on the search engine results pages (SERPs) to find the truly local solution to their problem or need. This is because Google, Yahoo and Bing all require the retailer or service provider to not only have a local physical location – but to prove it through a stringent process typically involving postcard verification through the US Mail.

Being setup and optimized for these is NOT the same thing as typical directory listings management such as for Merchant Circle and various online Yellow Pages. Getting placed in the Maps Sections takes a lot more work. It involves the actual claiming, verification and optimization of listings that appear in the map sections of the three largest search engines in the world.

The big player here is Google and they also happen to be the one who has made the most radical changes. That said; let's do a quick review of the evolution of their Google+ section...

June 2011 – The beta of Google+, or G+ as many call it, rolled out on this historic day. The demand was so overwhelming that it was stopped temporarily and then back in full swing for early September. According to Wikipedia, it reached 25 million users in the first 24 days of beta release on 6/28/2011.

For anyone who remembers *Google Buzz* or *Google Friend Connect*, Google+ was basically the next major step in Google's foray into social. This time however, Google developed a way to group family, friends, colleagues, and acquaintances into *circles*. Google+ also has a +1" button that most people familiar with Facebook, equate to a "like".

September 2011 – Google+ pushed the social envelope by allowing people to use their *Hangout* feature to host group meetings and gatherings. This technology was used by President Barack Obama to discuss the State of the Union on January 30, 2012.

November 2011 – Google+ Pages or "Business Pages" made it possible for businesses and organizations to stay more in touch with their followers, customers and potential customers. This is BIG part of local listing SEO success.

June 2012 – Google+ Events was integrated and allowed participants to add events and invite others to participate. It also allowed for sharing photos and other features available with Facebook.

June 2014 – Google decided to merge Google Places and Google+ Local Business Pages with "*Google My Business*". This is a logical next step but it took a lot of people by surprise.

Google My Business has the same interface look as Google+, which I think really helped people adapt easily However it also includes some slick new features such as insights and analytics that are catching on quickly.

In Closing: Google+, along with integrated features such as Google+ Pages, plays a major role in any company's online visibility regarding local search. Having a properly optimized Google+ listing should be a top priority.

Source Citation: We would like to thank Wikipedia.org

Note: With the July 24th 2014 Google Pigeon update everything is extremely local and based on quality like never before. Google+ is more important than ever, so optimize away!

PPC Update 2014

In the first edition of this book, we showed you how to get the most bang for your buck by taking advantage of all that Google offered in their AdWords campaigns. One of those considerations was the ability to place phone numbers in text ads.

As of March 2013 Google eliminated this option. They do, however, allow advertiser to use the "call extensions" feature. This is much larger conversation than we should tackle here, so here is Google's support doc:

https://support.google.com/adwords/answer /2453991?hl=en

"In the next few weeks, we will no longer allow phone numbers to be used in the ad text of new ads. Advertisers who would still like to promote phone numbers in their AdWords advertising can use the call extensions feature. We're posting this alert now to provide adequate lead time to make ad changes.

In April 2013, we will begin to disapprove ads that were using phone numbers in their ad text before the March 2013 policy change."

There have been other minor changes and even new product introduction (such as AdWords Express) but one of the greatest upsets has been the loss of ability to target mobile devises only in an AdWords campaign.

In early 2013, a year after this book's first edition, Google removed the ability to target to mobile devices only. This is a big deal because the alternative is something called AdWords Enhanced, which allows you to target mobile more specifically by increasing your bids on that platform – NOT by choosing on which device you want your ad to show.

Why the big deal over mobile? Matt Cutts, of Google, had a comment that should help answer that question…

While speaking at SMX West, in March of 2014, Matt Cutts stated that he "wouldn't be surprised" if mobile search exceeded desktop queries this year.

Now that's a big deal!

Worth Chatting About

Chat services for driving leads have been around for some time. We started working with several methods back in 2012 as add-ons for SEO and PPC services. Here's how it generally works…

You can have a live chat session with a potential or existing customer through an online chat window on your website. This is much like traditional chat or instant messaging dating back to the 1990's. But there's a twist.

You can either have one of your own representatives be available for chat or you can hire a chat service provider to be available for you. The latter is the preferred method for most people as it's basically the equivalent of an online answering service, without any of the negative connotations that often exist with getting a call service – especially in cases of emergency.

When you have a company handle your chat sessions for you, you provide a basic script meant to get you the warmest lead possible. The script can also include scenarios that determine nest steps, such as:

➢ Is the caller within your service area?
➢ Do you offer the service they need?
➢ Is this an emergency requiring immediate attention?
➢ Should the chat representative set up a call between you and the customer instantly?
➢ Should you call the client back at a certain time?

There are plenty of options to consider. The bottom-line is that chat can help people get much more engaged than simply completing a web form – and ask them to consider things they may not have otherwise considered.

Video Made the Internet Star

For anyone reading this who grew up in the 1980's, you probably remember MTV back when it actually played music videos. The very first video aired was a one-hit-wonder called "Video Killed the Radio Star". To a large degree, that prediction came true.

It makes sense. Why enjoy music with just one sense when you can see a three minute clip giving you the artist's perspective, or at the very least some entertaining visuals that help keep your attention.

That same logic works for product and service videos – as long as they are not commercials. Ah, therein lies the rub… "as long as they are not commercials".

So how do you make a video that explains the benefits you offer without it sounding like a commercial? It's called an "explainer video" and it can change your world!

"Explainers" are short videos that clarify or elaborate on one or more specific topics. They are typically compilations of any of the following; images, animations, text, music, voice narration, etc. – combined into a single medium, such as an MP4 or Flash movie.

But that's just the technical definition. The important thing is that explainer videos are attention-grabbing, crowd drawing, conversion making machines! It's not unusual for a single one-minute long video to significantly boost sales, attract thousands of new shoppers to a site and even bring in hundreds of backlinks from social channels.

Of course, it all depends on the type and topic of video, but even a simple one for a service industry business can greatly improve a visitor's interest factor, create a buzz and increase conversions.

Let's take a quick look at video types, what works where, and why they work…

Video Types

It's easy to confuse "type" with "style". For our purposes, "type" will describe the video's purpose and "style" will refer to its construction method.

Regarding types; there are as many as you can imagine. The standard types you most often see tend to be the more successful so we will focus our energies on these:

1. Sales Pitch
    a. Why Choose Us?
    b. What We Do
    c. How We Can Help
2. Savings
    a. Special Offers
    b. How We Save You Time
    c. How We Save You Money
3. Solid Reputation
    a. About Us

      b.   Company Résumé

      c.   Testimonials

4. Announcement

      a.   New Product

      b.   New Service

      c.   Special Event

5. How To; Instructional

      a.   How To (Step-by-Step)

      b.   Tutorials

      c.   Training

      d. Tips

6. Educational

      a.   Stats

      b.   Industry Information

      c.   Consumer Awareness

7. History

      a.   Advances and Developments

This is not meant to be a complete list, but rather an overview of the more common video types and samples of their purposes. Now let's look at video styles to get an idea of how the above concepts are portrayed.

Video Styles

There are many types of explainer videos with the following being most popular:

Cartoon

Cartoon style videos are among the hottest in 2014 and likely will be for years to come. Adults have been conditioned from childhood to associate cartoons with happiness. U.S. businesses are not allowed to use cartoons to advertise to children so there has never been a "sales" association with them.

This allows viewers to stay at ease and focus on your message. Speaking of focus, with cartoons nobody is looking at the petty details – but rather they see the bigger picture of the message. Better still; a little background music really sets the mood.

These are known for their very high quality and are among the most likely to "go viral" do to their fun-factor, timelessness and storytelling ability. "Viral", in this instance, equates to lots of free publicity and backlinks.

Animated Whiteboard

Animated Whiteboard videos are like "leads gold" in 2014. An updated version of the classic line-art hand-drawn effect whiteboard videos, the animated variation is relatively new to the scene and combines a proven medium with the wow factor of animation. Put in some background music or narrative, and you've got a lead-driving machine running on 24/7 auto-pilot.

Only a very small margin of success lies between cartoon style videos and animated whiteboard pieces. And, to be honest, I think it's due to price more than quality or results.

Storyboard Whiteboard

Storyboard style explainer videos have been around for some time. They use "stills" or still images, and can be accompanied by text and/or audio, all presented in a specific order. There is plenty you can do with them and these still work well when designed, developed and executed properly.

Article to Video

Among the quickest and least expensive to produce, article style videos are ideal for more detailed explainers where impressive graphics and effects are not critical to success.

Live Action

The original "video-taped" explainer videos predate YouTube by nearly a decade. While these can be effective in some instances, their over-use and common, everyday feel tend to make them seem more like cheap commercials unless they are extremely well done.

In Closing

If you have the opportunity to take advantage of explainer videos; don't hesitate.

Think Local; Act Mobile

Here are three things that can be done to help most websites become much more mobile SEO friendly - without requiring rollout on a grand scale to all franchisee sites; regardless of sub-domain or sub-directory structure:

First: Design one or more mobile formatted pages that automatically get shown when a mobile searcher visits your site. This is easily handled with small code snippets that show a particular page when a device attempts to access the site.

This might sound old-school, and it is, but it's also a good idea for any site to have at least one mobile-friendly page with contact info because "feature phones" cannot interpret responsive sites. And, in the US and UK, nearly half of all phones that look like smartphone, are actually just feature phones.

They let you access the Web, play games, and send texts and pics – but lack the computing power of a Smartphone.

According to Gartner.com, the gap is widening between smartphone and feature phone usage, with nearly 58% of new purchases going to smartphones in early 2014. But that's still billions of feature phones accessing websites every day.

Second: Take greater advantage of a Google+ Business Page. These can provide a great resource to any potential visitor and the page is mobile-friendly and hosted by Google. It doesn't get much better than that!

Third: Use shorter titles and descriptions in your Meta tags. It's no surprise that mobile devices don't display as much text as desktop computers but very few people design with that in mind. Well I have good news for anyone teetering on the fence about changing their title tag length... Google performed a SERP redesign in March 2014 that will help make the decision for you.

Without getting into the detail of fixed-width characters, use of capitalization and how it affects visible character count in the SERPs, I can provide some very simple guidelines.

The days of 65 to 72 character length title tags not being truncated are long gone. To be certain your entire title – and meaning – are recognized in the Search Engine Results Pages (SERPs), you should plan to use no more than 54 characters. If you can use as few as 49 and still get your message across, that's even better.

There are plenty of other things you can do to really embrace the mobile movement, but this information can make your site a contender without breaking the bank or taking months to implement.

Part One: Controlling the Message

What We All Want:

Following is just a reminder of what everyone wants in order to succeed when it comes to controlling the message.

Franchisors want...

✓ to control the message

In comparison, franchisees want...

✓ to control their own offers

This is almost always the first challenge we see in any new online marketing project, whether it be SEO, PPC, or Social Media. The ability to control the message is everyone's greatest desire, and most - if not all - other challenges stem from this one. Both the franchisor and the franchisee feel it is their right, and responsibility, to control the message.

Before we get into solutions, let's explore the challenge from the perspectives of both the franchisor and the franchisee - without bias for either.

Franchisor:

"Our message is our reputation. All it takes is one franchisee, or their blogger or marketing firm, to make one simple mistake or say the wrong thing and every franchisee will suffer from the fallout. Our big, profitable company's stock could become worth pennies overnight. It's happened to bigger fish than us."

Franchisee:

"How am I supposed to stand out from the local competition when I can't even represent my own company in my own words? It's bad enough that most people don't know the difference between a big box store and a franchise location like mine. It's hard for them to see me as a local businessperson, providing a great product at a fair price, when my hands are tied like this."

Experience:

We at NetSearch Direct have seen this, literally, more than a hundred times. And although it seems like the toughest challenge to overcome, it's actually pretty simple. There are a LOT of opportunities to send out a message that fits everyone's needs. All you need are some guidelines.

Let's take a look at options for each aspect of online marketing we are tackling: SEO, PPC and Social Media.

SEO

Challenge:

Most franchisors have a specific allowable block of text that just gets replicated a hundred times, once on each franchisee's page in the corporate site (or on micro-sites), with the only change being a simple swap of the city name. Some franchisors even have three or four blocks of text that franchisees can choose from. Although the second option is better, neither is very helpful from a search engine optimization perspective. The trouble is that search engines HATE duplicate content. And hate might not even be a strong enough word. If a search engine registers duplicate content on more than one page, it typically indexes just the first instance, meaning that all those duplicated pages won't show up in search engine results. And that's if you're lucky! Sometimes it will disallow ALL of the pages that carry the duplicate content. Simply switching out a city name that occupies 1 in 100 words of text will not make the content unique by search engine standards, so these methods are just trouble waiting to happen.

Step by Step Solution: SEO

Step 1: Multiple versions of approved franchisee text for the website (for each product or service description) are developed by an SEO copywriter (internal or external).

Step 2: A list of approved synonyms are developed and made available to franchisees for putting their own style and voice to the text. For example, "here's" might be acceptable to replace "here is" to handle conversational versus formal speech - or "amazing" or "great" could replace "beneficial" in order to modify descriptors.

Step 3: Acceptable parameters are set regarding things like total word count, length of page, use of location or geographic common names (for example, "Southie" for South Boston, Massachusetts, as it's called by residents).

Step 4: An image approval system is put in place that will allow franchisees to submit their own photos for approval, to be used in conjunction with the company's stock images. These would have to meet approved guidelines, and images involving clients or members would likely require signed photo releases. Yes, there is extra work here, but it can pay off in spades by putting a local face on the franchise.

Putting It All Together: SEO

Now the franchisee has all they need to combine paragraphs, add their own voice and style and come up with plenty of SEO-rich, unique text that the search engines will love. And their efforts will benefit the entire organization and ALL of the other franchisee pages on the website because they boost the overall site's value from a search engine perspective.

There is no expensive programming required for this. All of the text can be developed in any word processing software. The costs will be minimal and the results can pay off two-fold with good will between franchisor and franchisee as well as a multitude of leads from Google, Yahoo and Bing.

At NetSearch Direct, we have been using an advanced variation of this model (complex and effective enough that the technology is patent pending) to get top results for franchisors and franchisees across the United States and Canada. However, even in its simplest, manual form as outlined above, it produces great results.

Pay Per Click Advertising

Challenge:

There is actually more than one challenge here. The one we are concerned with is controlling the message, but the one that might put the kibosh on the whole thing is competition between the franchisor and franchisee.

You see, in PPC you are competing with everyone else that has placed a bid for a specific keyword - including the other franchisees and/or the franchisor (Corporate). This means you - and your fellow sharers of the brand - are driving up the cost for each other, depending on search perimeter (the radius in miles from your location - all the way out to national). If independent PPC campaigns are not allowed by your franchisor, this is probably the reason.

The following solution will take care of both challenges; 1.) controlling the message in PPC and 2.) limiting internal competition...

Step by Step Solution: PPC

Step 1: A list of keywords, eligible for bidding, is defined. This is with the understanding that the approved "GEO" name (city, town, state, etc.) can be added before or after the keyword by the franchisee - if they so wish.

For example, if your business is an auto repair shop located in Richmond, the keyword might be "Richmond auto repair".

Step 2: A maximum allowable geographic radius for the campaign to run is set. This will help prevent overlap between franchisees in nearby areas.

Most PPC platforms will allow you to set a radius in miles. Keeping with the example of an auto repair business, if your franchise territory covered cities within a 30 mile radius, we could safely select a 25 mile radius and have no fear of stepping into someone else's franchise area.

Word to the Wise

Some PPC opportunities offer exact cities as boundaries while others provide a radius in mileage (even easier!), while still others are a bit looser with estimated travel time. Google, for example, will have an advertiser select the radius in terms of definite distance, so make sure you and the franchisor agree to the exact terms before you begin.

Step 3: Standardized PPC ads, for each keyword in the approved list, are developed and banked for access and use by franchisees. Again, these can be modified by the franchisee to include the GEO name.

Important Note: *A big part of PPC that people often forget about is having a custom landing page* instead of depending on the regular website pages.*

Word Opp:

Landing Page: This is simply a single web page put in place for the sole purpose of having a user go directly to it - rather than, say - the home page. In PPC this can be very valuable because it allows you to cater a page's look, feel, and content for an exact theme or keyword. That helps a great deal with converting visitors to purchasers.

Step 4: Several possible PPC landing pages are developed and made accessible to franchisees. There should be at least two versions of each: one with no mention of the GEO, another with a spot to replace [GEO] with the actual town, city or state name.

Step 5: Before we close out of this section it is important to note that PPC actually has two messages to control: that on the landing page and the ad itself. When creating your ads for Google, Bing and Yahoo, the franchisor will have to take into consideration their own standards and requirements, then get that same ad approved by Corporate. This is a very important consideration.

For an auto glass business it might be something like:

Auto Glass From $99.00

www.WindshieldInstall.com
Affordable Windshield/Auto Glass
installed nationwide, Instant Quote

The ad above is not a great one, so I'll show you how to improve it in the next section.

Note: *This is a good time to mention that PPC does not rely on unique content, so having standard and duplicate ads works quite well.*

Putting It All Together: PPC

This system allows control of the message for the franchisor with enough flexibility to make the message work well for the franchisee, not to mention some creative control in the ad selection and landing page type. At the same time, this helps build brand awareness, which will benefit the franchisor as well.

Take Note

You might ask, "Why use landing pages instead of a page on the main site?", and it's a good question. It all comes down to something known as "quality score". In the world of search engines, Quality Score is determined by a complex algorithm* that applies a whole bunch of values to a page, based on things like the text on the page, how often a specific keyword appears, where the keyword appears throughout the page, how long a visitor stays on that page, and so on. If you had to worry about all of these tiny details on *your regular web pages, you'd be limiting each page to just one keyword or keyword theme. That could make for a lot of extra work and potentially hurt your overall SEO at the same time. This makes the landing page an ideal solution, since your purpose is to limit the page to just one keyword theme**.*

** Keyword themes are a device NetSearch uses to eliminate restrictions otherwise common to keyword selection. A theme uses a strong search term as a base with many similar terms optimized in the SEO process. This often improves ROI by 2 and 3 fold.

Word Opp:

Algorithm: For our simple needs, an algorithm can be best defined as a process driven by a formula. You can think of it as a recipe, where the cooking instructions are the process and the list of ingredients is the formula.

Social Media

Challenge:

The big challenge with social media, when it comes to controlling the message, is that **"anything you say can and will be re-tweeted."**

Yes, that's an exaggeration but certainly a possibility. In fact, it's your GOAL. Just understand the following distinction:

Social media is all about getting people talking about you or your business.

Social media *marketing* is all about getting people talking about you or your business in the best possible light.

Can You Relate?

Consider this scenario and its three variations:

You stop for your morning coffee and the person behind the counter...

1.) ...slides your coffee across the counter to you and says, "Sleeves are there. Napkins are there. Thanks. Next."

2.) ...places the perfect cup in front of you, fixed exactly the way you like it - already with a protective cardboard heat sleeve in place and two napkins placed neatly beside it. With a big smile on her face, she says in a friendly manner, "That was a medium hazelnut with one sugar and a dash of cream. Is that correct? Excellent! Great to see you this morning, please come back."

3.) ...slides your coffee across the counter with a loose lid so it sloshes over and runs down the side of the cup. You ask for a napkin to wipe the cup and she points at a stack on the far end of the counter. You ask for a cardboard sleeve and she says "over there" while making an impatient hand gesture vaguely in the direction of the napkins. You open your mouth to say thank you and before you can get a word out she says, "Do you still need something? I've got other customers you know!"

If you are like most people, scenario number one was just business as usual and not really worth the time or effort for you to talk about. Scenario two was wonderful, but be honest - how many people are you going to bother to tell? You will likely tell only those people who you believe will genuinely care. Scenario three on the other hand was just bad enough that it's worth mentioning to a few people.

Now, here's where it gets interesting. Other people who hear about the third situation will likely feel compelled to mention it to their friends - and possibly "improve" it along the way. By the time you leave work that evening, there's a good chance you will overhear a conversation like this: "Did you hear that nasty piece of work at the coffee shop threw a cup of coffee at some guy this morning?"

You've seen it before and maybe even taken part in some way. Now take the above situation and multiply it by one thousand. That's the power of social media - for better or worse. As you can see, sending out the right message is key. The good coffee place will have its praises sung amongst the niche group of people who are interested, while tales of the bad one will be heard by everyone within shouting range.

You might be saying, "I want to market my business, not throw coffee at some guy." True enough. But have you considered how fast and far something in writing can spread? The coffee story is hearsay and would likely be urban legend within a few weeks, but a posting to Facebook or tweet on Twitter has more staying power. Of course, this is what you want - marketing longevity.

Social Media: The Good, The Bad, and The Solution

Before we go on, I would like to add a very short section with examples of both a social media success and a social media bomb. These are tweets and posts made by multi-billion dollar companies with plenty of concerned franchise owners that demonstrate polar opposite, true, unbiased, examples of the best and worst-case scenarios.

The Good

There are many examples of great successes we could pull from but let's choose an American auto manufacturer who made history with their use of Facebook. Back in 2010, Ford Motor Company decided to host the 2011 Ford Explorer model release via Facebook rather than at a "showplace event" as was the custom. This was a first in history for any major auto manufacturer - and it paid off BIG.

It was a totally original event that brought in the biggest, and most interactive, group of genuinely interested spectators in the company's one hundred seven year history. Talk about a social media success!

I won't use up too much space here describing all they did. You can Google that. But I will say that there were interactive opportunities that converted 'merely interested' spectators into long-term Ford evangelists.

The Bad

Sticking with major auto brands, let's look at Chrysler. In 2011, this little gem came out on their Twitter feed:

"I find it ironic that Detroit is known as the motorcity and yet no one here knows how to f@&*ing drive" [expletive filtered]

Google this now and you'll find a ton of articles still hanging out there on the internet about this, the perfect example of how an inexpertly managed social media program can turn around and bite you. But it doesn't have to be this way.

The Solution

Not participating in social media marketing because someone made a mistake, at a company you do not even work for, would be a bit extreme. There is "cautious" and then there is "inviting your competition to eat your lunch".

Social media marketing does not have to be about setting records and reaching a million new people in one epic effort. In fact, the original Webster's Dictionary definition of marketing was "To keep one's name in the public eye." We could even take that a step further and say "To keep one's name and message in the public eye." Social media marketing's simplest use is just that: a way to keep existing customers engaged and attract new ones with your message. It's a great way to keep everyone informed with minimal investments of time or money.

...take that a step further and say "To keep one's name and message in the public eye."

That said, the best way to minimize risk and maximize reward is to follow a carefully planned social media strategy like this...

Step by Step Solution: Social

Step 1: One or more desired social media outlets are selected, based on franchisee nomination. Facebook and Twitter are great places to start given their popularity. Google+, still being tweaked, is another one to keep an eye on.

Step 2: Optional - Corporate profiles and/or pages are implemented for the selected outlets. If this step is taken, there should be a commitment to at least three posts per week.

Note: *The above optional step is meant for Corporate only, although any design work can be implemented in Step 3 below for individual franchisees.*

Step 3: An approved page, theme, or background is developed for each outlet by the franchisor, for use by all interested franchisors.

Step 4: A 'message pool' for each social media outlet is developed and implemented. This will invite participating franchisees to select from approved messages that are already the correct length and type for Facebook, Twitter, etc. To maximize flexibility, steps 2 and 3 from the SEO section of Part One can be implemented as well. I'll repeat them here for your convenience:

> **SEO Step 2:** Provide a list of approved synonyms such as "here's" to replace "here is" to handle conversational versus formal speech - or "amazing" or "great" to replace "beneficial" to modify descriptors.

> **SEO Step 3:** Set the acceptable parameters regarding things like total word count, length of page, if location-common names can be used (like "Southie" for South Boston, Massachusetts, as it is called by residents).

Putting It All Together: Social

The aforementioned solution allows the franchisee to help spread the word with some local flair while the franchisor has an easy way to make sure the message being touted is the one desired.

This concept is ideally suited to contests as well - especially if any of the prizes to be awarded are on a local level.

How could you put this to work for you?

Part One Summary

The only reason the franchisor or the franchisee wants to control the message is so they can be sure the right message is going out.

Again, really understanding that franchisors and franchisees are both on the same team - and can see things from both perspectives - makes it a lot easier to find a solution that works well for everyone. Better still, the solution will ensure not only that the right message is going out, but also that its being spread farther and wider than ever before.

Now that's a win-win!

Part Two: Branding/Marketing Flexibility

What We All Want:

Again, just a reminder of what everyone wants in order to succeed when dealing with Branding/Marketing Flexibility.

Franchisors want...

✓ to protect the brand

In comparison, franchisees want...

✓ marketing and advertising flexibility

This is a challenge that likely erupted about ten minutes after the very first franchise was created. The franchisor wants to protect the brand, usually by maintaining full control, while the franchisee wants to have maximum flexibility with regard to marketing and advertising. And this goes a lot deeper than use of logos and making sure the company colors are right, although those can both be big parts.

Franchisor:

"Our brand is our bread and butter. It's how people recognize us instantly and associate all the good things we can do for them. We have brought in experts and paid a fortune to develop the right logo, color scheme, sales-marks, trademarks, slogans and taglines. Displaying anything wrong just one time can undo the work and expense that went into showing the brand perfectly one thousand times before."

Franchisee:

"I paid a lot to represent this brand and I want to get as much out of it as possible. I just need to do some extra marketing and advertising to drive in business. I'm not some idiot that's going to do something that makes us look bad."

Experience:

Of every aspect of franchisor and franchisee online marketing, this is where we tend to see the most discrepancy. The franchisor has often invested millions of dollars in building the brand. They have hired experts to help select the right look and feel, and even the smallest change can alter the desired effect.

To really understand this, let's look at three of the simplest aspects that most of us take for granted:

1. color
2. typeface
3. slogans

The Color of Branding

Here are some examples of how even simple shades of colors can mean the difference between success and failure in setting the right tone. Have you ever heard of...

"Coca-Cola Red"?

"UPS Brown"?

"Home Depot Orange"?

Those are among the most familiar companies that have a "color-mark" protecting their shades. But there are plenty of others. What about "Cadbury Purple" and "T-Mobile Magenta"? Here's one you have probably seen in hundreds of places you never even imag-ined - "Barbie Pink". It's used in everything from bubblegum to breakfast cereals and that shade is worth millions!

How robust is the protection of these shades? How's this for starters...

UPS is suing (ironically enough) a lawyer named "Brown" for using a shade of brown that they feel is too close to theirs.

T-Mobile has gone after a number of companies that they feel are infringing on their shade of magenta - reportedly even for companies doing business in areas where the color-mark is not legally binding!

And let's not even get into the hundreds of lawsuits that have resulted from other brands who felt violated - lawsuits that have racked up millions of dollars in legal fees and hundreds of hours in our courts.

Color Me Confused

So how does this affect a franchisee who just needs to do a little extra marketing? It's like this: basically every piece of collateral* that you DON'T get from the franchisor is a potential problem because it can "dilute the brand" or even undermine its recognition as a defensible aspect of the brand.

Consider what goes into the process as far as proof when applying for a patent or trademark - aside from tens or even hundreds of thousands of dollars. The color "Cadbury Purple", for example, required more than ten years of lobbying efforts before it was considered a defensible aspect of the brand. Cadbury had to prove that the color was synonymous with the brand and any use of "off colors" during that long defense process (or even before it) could have sunk the deal. Then what would have become of the bunny who clucks like a chicken?

Back to the question at hand, "So how does this affect a franchisee that just needs to do a little extra marketing?"

If a franchisee develops an unauthorized website that does not use the right colors, it can undermine the tremendous effort, time, and expense that went into establishing the colors of the brand. The same can be said of using a poor quality copy of the logo or showing the wrong typefaces or any of a hundred additional considerations that may seem trivial on the outside but make the brand what it is - and what the franchisee paid to represent.

Of course, the website is just one example - but it's the most common, followed closely by blog, Facebook page, and Twitter feed. We will get more into the nitty-gritty of this in the

next section dealing with independent websites. For now let's just focus on the issue of
color itself.

Word Opp:

Collateral: Simply put, this
is any sketched, written,
recorded, electronic or other
"media" used to support
sales, or more specifically,
a sales campaign. Consider it
an accumulation of marketing
material. Everything from the
humble brochure to the mighty
Super Bowl commercial is
considered marketing collateral for a given sales campaign.

Typecast Typefaces

You might think of a typeface as just another font you can find installed on your computer, but it is actually much more and has multiple levels of protection available, such as:

1. Trademark
2. Copyright
3. Patent
4. Trade Secret
5. Ethics

The most common protection you encounter on a day-to-day basis surrounds the design patent, defining and protecting how the typeface appears physically. Think of the "C" in Coca-Cola™ for a minute. Can you see it clearly in your mind? Ask the majority of people in any developed country that the U.S. does business with and they will answer "Yes". That's the power of the brand!

Trading on Trademarks

The last of the big three that we will explore with regard to branding is the trademark - and lumped, unceremoniously in with it - copyright, slogans, and sales-marks. We are basically talking about any text that helps define a brand.

Consider for a moment Nike's famous "Just Do It" campaign, still legendary after its introduction more than twenty-five years ago. Building a brand like that takes a lot of work and a whole lot of money. Now imagine if one hundred shoe store owners decided to tweak that with their own "original flair". It might go something like this...

"Just go ahead and do it."
"We've got the sneakers. You just do it."
"Do it now."

Or any of a hundred even worse variations. Farfetched? You'd be surprised. In fact, it can get even worse. I will illustrate with a slight variation of one that my SEO manager ran into about thirteen years ago. The client was a beauty and massage spa whose slogan was...

"A day of beauty; the best conclusion to any week" *(modified from original to protect company identity).*

Okay, that sounds promising. But the version created by one branch who wanted to fill massage tables made an even bigger promise with...

"Massage; get a happy ending to your day here".

Apparently someone with just a little bit of marketing brainpower wanted to capitalize on a very popular keyword without really understanding what it implied.

SEO

Challenge:

From an SEO perspective, color and logo will almost never be an issue, but anything in writing is a potential victim. But not to worry, there is a very simple SEO solution that we'll get into in a minute. First however, let's give ourselves a ground rule regarding color schemes and logo usage:

Regardless of what other steps are taken, the franchisor should always supply approved templates and/or have a simple approval process in place. By the same token, franchisees should always use approved materials and follow process.

Okay, now we can get into the solution, some of which will look familiar...

Step by Step Solution: SEO

Step 1: SEO Guidelines are developed that include a list of approved - and disallowed keywords. There can also be an approval process as the final stage for this, or any of the following steps.

Step 2: A list of approved synonyms are developed and made available to franchisees for putting their own style and voice to the message. For example, the term "you're" might be acceptable to replace "you are" to handle conversational versus formal speech - or "incredible" or "fantastic" could replace "very good" in order to modify descriptors.

Step 3: Acceptable parameters are set regarding things like total word count, length of page, use of location common names (for example, "The Village" for Greenwich Village in New York).

Step 4: An image approval system is put in place that will allow franchisees to submit their own photos for approval, to be used in conjunction with the company's stock images. These would have to meet approved guidelines, and images involving clients or members would likely require signed photo releases. Yes, there is extra work here, but it can pay off in spades by putting a local face on the franchise.

Putting It All Together: SEO

In general, consumers like to do business locally. "Think. Shop. Buy Local" has become the battle cry of American small business and Joe Consumer does not always understand that franchise stores and offices are owned and operated by local people just like him. The above solution makes the brand mean more at a local level without risking brand integrity.

The right SEO solution makes the total franchise brand mean more at a local level - without risking brand integrity.

Pay Per Click Advertising

Challenge:

Although the keyword concerns will be very similar to those in SEO, PPC also has another major consideration...

The landing page must meet the Corporate branding criteria.

Step by Step Solution: PPC

Step 1: PPC Guidelines are developed to include a list of approved and non-approved keywords for bidding. As in "Controlling the Message", these could include GEO names and acceptable advertising radiuses.

Step 2: An approved landing page template is provided by Corporate. Failing that, the landing page design and color scheme must be approved by Corporate prior to launch.

Step 3: Guidelines are set regarding criteria such as acceptable advertising networks.

Note: *Many PPC campaigns run on other independent websites - not just the search engine - if you so choose. You have probably visited websites that include a section of Google ads in the sidebar or at the bottom of the page. These sites are part of the networks that can be avoided or included.*

Step 4: In an effort to add a local flavor, the franchisor may add in any approved local testimonials or images.

Step 5: We covered this in "Controlling the Message" but it bears repeating. PPC actually has two messages to control, as follow:

1. the message presented on the landing page
2. the message within the ad itself

When creating your ad for Google, Bing and Yahoo, the franchisor will have to deal with their standards and requirements and then get that same ad approved by Corporate. This is a very important consideration.

Putting It All Together: PPC

The same considerations that we discussed for SEO apply here as well. I have repeated it for your convenience. In general, consumers like to do business locally. "Think. Shop. Buy Local" has become the battle cry of American small business and Joe Consumer does not always understand that franchise stores and offices are owned and operated by local people just like him. The above solution makes the brand mean more at a local level without risking brand integrity.

Taking this concept one step further, it is even easier to perfect your message with PPC than with SEO. With PPC you can anticipate how many visits you will get depending on your ad copy and the ad position for which you have bid. This means that you can plan to have one hundred visits and then tweak the landing page (within approved parameters) for the next one hundred, to see which provides the better conversion rate.

And speaking of perfecting the message... Don't forget about your opportunity to tweak the advertising message within the ad itself - including the offer.

If you originally had:

Auto Glass from $99.00
www.WindshieldInstall.com
Affordable Windshield/Auto Glass
installed nationwide, Instant Quote

And you got a 1% click through rate, you might try something like:

Windshields from $99.00
www.WindshieldInstall.com
Affordable Windshield/Auto Glass
installed in Richmond. Visit today!

Chances are this will bring in much better results.

Here is what we did...

First of all we put the exact keyword "windshield" instead of the generic "auto glass".

Next, we let them know that the new windshield is replaced where they live and work. They do not care if you install windshields nationwide. They care about LOCAL service and reputation.

And finally, we have added a call to action with "Visit today!"

The AdWords rules can be a bit tricky so it's worth the time to check their AdWords Policy section before investing a lot of time in ad development.

https://support.google.com/adwordspolicy/

PPC Bonus

Although that might simply look like a PPC bonus section on writing an ad that converts better, it is far more. In fact, keep that little ad in mind for the remainder of this book because it is applicable in every future section as well.

As for how it relates to Branding/Marketing Flexibility, that's easy. Careful wording protects the brand, while gaining increased targeted visitors magnifies brand awareness. The "marketing flexibility", of course, is a bit more obvious.

Social Media

Challenge:

As we recently learned, controlling the message with social media is extremely important due to its likelihood of spreading. The same can be said of protecting the brand.

Although marketing flexibility is important, careful guidelines and procedures should be followed to ensure the brand is not compromised in any way.

Step by Step Solution: Social

Step 1: If not already addressed from "Controlling the Message", one or more desired social media outlets are selected, based on franchisee nomination. Facebook and Twitter are great places to start, given their popularity. Google+, still being tweaked, is another one to keep an eye on.

Step 2: With a special eye for ensuring the color scheme, typefaces, images and logo are protected; an approved page, theme, or background is developed by the franchisor, for use by all interested franchisees.

Step 3: The 'message pool', created in the last section for each social media outlet is further developed to include additional brand-specific notices that will benefit both the franchisee and the franchisor. Once again, this will invite participating franchisees to select from approved messages that are already the correct length and type for Facebook, Twitter, etc.

Branding Bonus

What do I mean by "brand-specific" notices? These will be posts and tweets specific to Corporate news that can be modified to include relevant regional facts the local followers would find interesting.

For example, a news release about how the franchise is celebrating its twenty-fifth anniversary is certainly big news for the company but it does not really pass the "Who cares?" test from Joe Public's point of view.

Now, take that same information and tie in a note like this:

"And to thank our loyal Boston customers, all sandwiches are buy-one/get-one free on Friday, August 22nd."

Now Joe <u>and all of his friends</u> will care.

Putting It All Together: Social

With a little compromise and some careful collaboration, the resulting product of branding through Social Media is greater than the sum of its individual components - far greater, if done properly. This is too great an opportunity to ignore.

"...the resulting product of branding through Social Media is greater than the sum of its individual components..."

Part Two Summary

Branding is something that most franchise organizations pay big money to accomplish. The stronger the brand, the better their chances of helping their franchisees do a good business as well as getting new franchisees to join the ranks. By the same token, marketing flexibility is extremely important to the franchisee that knows what it takes to succeed in his or her area - and is willing to do what it takes.

By implementing the solutions discussed in this section, both franchisor and franchisee can gain more than either ever dreamed possible, without either having to make sacrifices or pay for more than the value received.

Part Three: Managing the Web Presence

What We All Want:

You knew it was coming; a reminder of what everyone wants in order to succeed with regard to managing the web presence - be it independently or on the whole.

Franchisors want...

✓ to manage the web presence

In comparison, franchisees want...

✓ to control their own web presence

Here's one that has flip-flopped over the years. In the mid to late 1990's most franchisees were ecstatic at the thought of having a company web page without having to do anything. The web was new and just a place to display a simple "online brochure" that did little more than show a picture or two and provide store location and hours. By the early 2000's, these same business owners were seeing new potential and thus began an itch for web independence. Flash forward to present day and many savvy business owners are looking to integrate customer testimonials, video, audio, RSS feeds, live mobile uploads, QR codes, surveys, games and more.

This obviously has the potential to cause some tension between franchisors and franchisees. With so many opportunities to build out a website, there comes just as much opportunity to potentially cause problems, so let's explore the challenge from each perspective, as always, without bias for either.

Franchisor:

"We have a gorgeous website that cost a lot of money to build and takes a great deal of effort to keep up to date. It's not as easy as everyone thinks. Working with the 'web-safe' color palette was a bear to get our look just right, and turning our custom typefaces into images so they don't swap out to something completely wrong on the user's computer was a big task. And speaking of looking right, testing and tweaking for every (even somewhat recent) year of every notable web browser was a nightmare - but it's what we had to do to ensure that everything will show properly on all computers."

Franchisee:

"Sure the site looks good but it's just not converting. I need to add some neighborhood flavor like testimonials from locals and site surveys to get everyone really involved. And pictures! I need pictures of MY shop and MY staff and maybe a few of MY customers. I'd really like my own website to drive in leads."

Experience:

This is very common and, to be honest, one of the more complex situations we run into. Whether you are a franchisor or a franchisee, when you see it from the other's perspective it's kind of hard to just brush it off. All of those points are valid, but not to worry - we have a solution. Actually, for this one, we have several.

SEO

Challenge:

Here we step outside the realm of what most SEO companies consider their responsibility. At NetSearch Direct we pride ourselves on delivering Conversion Based SEO™, so much so that we have trademarked the term and made it our core offering. I mention this only because it gets straight to the heart of this particular issue and I am happy to be uniquely qualified to address it.

As we learned long ago, getting a web page to the top of a search engine for a particular keyword is not enough. Visitors are not enough. You need targeted visitors who are prime candidates to become paying clients. And attracting those future customers is an art and science in and of itself.

Now, unique to this situation we have two likely scenarios as follow:

Scenario One: The franchisor offers a single corporate site with one page set aside for each franchisee, which may or may not allow for independent updates. This is typically set up as a simple page arrangement as follows: main-site.com/franchisee-page.html

Scenario Two: The franchisor offers a single corporate site with individual micro-sites for each franchisee, which may or may not allow for independent updates. These micro-sites generally have more than one page and exist in a sub-domain (micro-site.main-site.com) or as a sub-directory (main-site.com/micro-site/).

In either scenario, the solution can be the same.

Step by Step Solution: SEO - One

Step 1: The top five requested add-on features are evaluated by Corporate to determine which are feasible within the current budget.

Step 2: Of those, as many as can be put into place for the available budget are voted on by the franchisees, one vote per location. For example:

Option One - 1.) Upload up to 5 images; 2.) Upload up to 10 text testimonials

Option Two - 1.) Upload up to three video testimonials

Option Three - 1.) Choose from 1 of 3 available surveys; 2.) Upload up to 5 images

Option Four - 1.) Choose from 1 of 3 available surveys; 2.) Upload up to 10 text testimonials

Step 3: After the votes are tallied, Corporate notifies all franchisees, provides release date estimates, training dates, and initiates the project.

Step 4: Guidelines for each feature are provided to all franchisees. For example, if one of the features selected was "Upload up to five images", the guidelines may be as follows...

Feature: Upload Up To Five Images

Guidelines: Each image must:

1. Be exactly 480 pixels wide by 240 pixels high (other sizes will not be compressed or stretched to fit this size, as it may adversely alter the appearance)

2. Be saved in standard ".jpg" or ".gif" or ".tiff" formats

3. Not exceed 400K in size per image

4. Not include any persons who have not signed the standard photo release

5. Fit the acceptability standards guidelines as outlined in the Acceptability Standards Guidelines document

6. Pass the review process set in place by Corporate

This, of course, is just an example but keep in mind that such requirements and guidelines are key to ensuring maximum effectiveness with minimum risk.

Wait! There's More:

This should take care of situations where the franchisee is agreeable with the Corporate site, as long as it is modified to help promote conversions, but there's an even bigger picture here. What about those franchisees who want, above all, their own website? Never fear, we have a few solutions for that as well. And at least one should work well for both franchisees and franchisors.

Step by Step Solution: SEO - Two

Step 1: Corporate develops a template that incorporates a series of the most in-demand features requested as well as a person, committee or other governing body to facilitate oversight and answer any questions.

Please note that this may be an agreeable solution only if enough franchisees commit to purchasing the template.

Step 2: A list of approved hosting environments, companies and plans is provided for the franchisee to choose from.

Step 3: The franchisee pays the set fee for the template and has it installed on one of the approved hosting environments.

Step 4: The franchisee follows the guidelines presented in "Controlling the Message" to add qualified, unique, SEO content to the site. Approved SEO techniques must also be followed to ensure there is no accidental cross-contamination of the brand.

Step 5: The franchisee provides the dev site* URL*, complete with SEO edits, to the franchisor approval committee.

Word Opp:

Dev Site: This is a shortened form of "Development Website" and refers to a website in any stage of development that has not yet been released for public access. It may reside on a closed/private web server or have code-based restrictions in place to stop the public from accessing it.

Word Opp:

URL: This acronym stands for "Uniform Resource Locator", an almost entirely unhelpful term. In more practical terms, this means the address of a site or page, usually found or typed into a box at the top of a browser ("http://www.netsearchdirect.com/", for example).

Step by Step Solution: SEO - Three

Step 1: Corporate provides a list of approved Web developers and SEO companies that have already signed-off on allowable designs and SEO methodologies.

Step 2: The franchisee works independently with the Web and SEO developer to build exactly what is needed, within the approved guidelines.

Step 3: The Web/SEO company gains franchisee approval and then submits the finished dev site with SEO edits to the franchisor for Corporate approval.

The previous three solutions work extremely well in almost any situation, but we have found a hybrid solution that appeals to many, as it involves developing a website, shared by multiple franchisees, that focuses on obtaining leads for all represented on the site. In fact, NetSearch has had such success with this concept; we have developed a technology to accommodate it called "Hyper Local" (US Patent Pending).

Following is a solution based on this concept that will work whether Hyper Local is used or not...

Step by Step Solution: SEO - Four

Step 1: A group of franchisees unite, pooling their resources, to have a lead generating website developed and optimized.

Note: A Corporate approved website is planned and developed, without any additional expense to Corporate.

Step 2: The website is developed containing the conversion factors most desired by the franchisees. At this stage it is helpful to use a development/SEO company that has some degree of expertise and experience in these matters to offer original solutions.

Note: To overcome buyer concerns for one major US based franchise, NetSearch developed a "customer locator" feature and implemented it into Hyper Local. This feature allows any site visitor to enter their zip code and then view a map that has pinpoints for every customer within that zip code (based on approximate address to protect individual customer identities). Conversions increased by 70% with this one simple tool - and that's just the start!

Step 3: The site is optimized for those search terms (keywords) most likely to result in a conversion.

Note: *Be sure your SEO company monitors this closely. Search patterns change more frequently than ever now that Google has implemented some of its more advanced search features. In addition, if they are using analytics as they should, they can even identify the exact search terms that convert the best.*

Step 4: The development company works with the franchisee group to facilitate the addition of other franchise territories.

Note: *This is an opportunity for the original investors to recoup some of their initial investments. I* *recommend having an agreement in place that stipulates each new territory signed will have their set-up fee divided between actual site development/SEO as well as income to those who made the initial investment. With enough new franchisee members, the entire leads site can be free (or close) for those who made it happen.*

"With enough new franchisee members, the entire leads site can be free (or close) for those who made it happen."

Putting It All Together: SEO

The name of the game here is options, and franchisee or franchisor; you've got a lot of them. The one that has worked extremely well for multiple situations is Number Four, the hybrid approach. This might be something to consider if the others do not seem promising for your exact situation.

PPC and Social Media

This section is about managing one's own web presence. Although this can be discussed within the context of PPC and Social Media, it is not really direct enough to warrant large sections of data because you already know most of it from previous sections. That said, I won't waste your time by repeating what we have already covered in the first two sections. Instead, I will just add a couple of notes you should carefully consider.

PPC

The only real web presence we need to worry about in PPC is that of the landing page(s). Again, we have covered this in great detail in both "Controlling the Message" and "Branding/Marketing Flexibility". I will simply say that once the right method has been put in place for franchisees to develop their own landing page content, the ability to make beneficial updates is not a tremendous leap. A condition allowing for such can simply be added to the program or programs resulting from "Controlling the Message" and "Branding/Marketing Flexibility".

Social Media

Take the same concept from PPC, immediately above, and apply it to any Facebook pages or Twitter posts that might be part of the newly developed Social Media strategy.

Part Three Summary

Managing the web presence combines the best and most complex aspects of controlling the message, branding and the desire for marketing flexibility. This can easily be a win-win for both franchisor and franchisee with a little careful planning and proper implementation. Again, there are a lot of choices available.

Part Four: Location, Location, Location

What We All Want:

One more time... A gentle reminder of what everyone wants in order to succeed when it comes to showing up for localities.

Franchisors want...

✓ to appeal to multiple geographical markets (parts of the state, country or even world)

In comparison, franchisees want...

✓ to show up locally on Google, Yahoo and Bing

Being found in the areas desired is, of course, key to your success - whether you are looking at it from the franchisee's or franchisor's perspective. Speaking of perspectives, let's take a look at each.

Franchisor:

"Our website has to attract business from all over, including those areas where we have franchises in place as well as those territories we need to fill. But it's expensive! We need to attract new franchisees to keep our overhead costs in check. And it's just too much work to try to show up for everything that everyone wants. Isn't 'Richmond' enough for that franchisee? Do they really need 'Chesterfield', 'Hanover', 'Midlothian', 'Henrico' and 'Short Pump'? What the heck is 'Short Pump' anyway?"

Franchisee:

"I need to show up on the search engines for what local folks are really searching for. It's great that the Corporate site tries to help me get leads for 'Richmond' but that's only a small part of my area. I want to capitalize on all of the local search coming in for 'Short Pump' now that over a billion dollars has been invested in making it the shopping 'go-to' place of Central Virginia. And for that matter, I'm lucky if I get one hundred visitors a month through that site. I need three hundred targeted visitors - at least 3% of which who will convert - just to break even."

Experience:

I have dealt with this many, many times over the years. There are some great solutions that are easy to implement at a minimal cost. Of all challenges so far, this is likely the easiest for those with the correct foundation in place (which I find to be the case 98% of the time or more).

So let's get down to some serious solutions...

SEO

Challenge:

The ability to show up locally for any given keyword search is a huge part of online marketing. This is especially true in any search engine that uses a map with pins to indicate your location and places that map above the regular search results. Sound familiar? You guessed it - Google.

Most major search engines have such a place reserved just for claimed and verified local listings. For Google it is known as Google Place Search (or Google Places, Google Maps or Google Local Listings, depending on who and when you ask).

So how do you take full advantage of beating out your local competition? Get into Google Places, of course! I know, I know. If it were that easy you would have already done it. It would take a book much bigger than this to explain all of the intricacies to extract the maximum benefit. In all honesty, it's not terribly difficult - after you have done a bunch - but it is well worth either trying on your own or hiring an expert to do it for you.

Going Places: Revisited

You might recognize the following from the first edition, but there's a nice little update at the end... With Place Search (Google Places), Google is going a step further in the march toward becoming THE local search engine. They accomplish this by simply integrating the old Google Places info into the regular search results - but not always grouped in the traditional "7-pack" most people are used to seeing. It's really pretty brilliant. They shake up the industry and appear to present entirely new rankings, using their old data. This, of course, ends up trumping some long-standing top placers and it all goes back to good old Google Places.

Word Opp:

7-Pack: Google's grouping of seven local search results at

```
the top of the first page of
results.
```

This is serious stuff, especially for those who have built a national online sales strategy that might now be invisible to sixty percent of the target market because of Google's 2011 changes, changes made to provide the most relevant local search results. But, then again, it's IDEAL for franchisors and franchisees that can reap the benefits from both sides.

Get ready for **Google My Business**!

For some good overall general information read the following section called "**Been There; Done That Again**". If you want the full scoop on the history of, well, let's just call it *Google Maps* shall we? Please check out the section called **Google+, Maps, and Local Listings** beginning on page 38. There you will find an historic overview with dates and innovations.

Been There; Done That Again

In our first edition we explained how, in 2011, Google has its Place Search/Google Places to narrow its focus on a smaller radius of search results in organic search. Following that update, the order in which your listing appeared had as much to do with where your business was physically located, in relation to where the search originated.

Flash forward to June 11, 2014 when Google decided to merge Google Places and Google+ Local Business Pages with "*Google My Business*". This really was the next logical step but it took a lot of people by surprise.

Google My Business has the same interface look as Google+, which I think really helped people adapt easily However it also includes some slick new features such as insights and analytics that are catching on quickly.

In short, to obtain page one rankings for local keyword phrases on Google, one must integrate a successful **Google+/Google My Business** strategy into their SEO plan. And that's just what our SEO Step by Step Solution will do.

Step by Step Solution: SEO

Step 1: Commit to inclusion in the various local listings sections for at least:

1. Google
2. Bing
3. Yahoo!

Step 2: Gather the following data/collateral, as you will need them for inclusion whether you do it on your own or hire an expert:

Business Name, Department, Address (only street addresses are accepted - no post office boxes), City, State, Zip, Local Number, Toll Free Number, Fax Number, Business Categories (you need **at least** three), Website, Email, Brands, Products/Services, Year Established, Hours of Operation, Languages Spoken, Payment Methods, Tagline, Logo Link (wherever it is stored on the Internet)

Step 3: Gather up to ten images you would like to be displayed. Resizing and formatting may be required, depending on the outlets selected.

Step 4: Decide if you will do it yourself or hire a professional.

Note: *Again it is not difficult once you are properly trained. NetSearch Direct has set up more than 2,000 such accounts over the past five years (about 700 each on Google, Yahoo! and Bing), roughly 100 of which were partially set up by the owners and sent to us for completion. In other words, if you want to give it a go on your own, many people have done so successfully and still others just needed help to get them ranking better.*

Putting It All Together: SEO

Getting your web presence listed prominently in search engine local listings is one of the best and lowest-cost online marketing investments you can make.

NetSearch does this as part of our SEO programs for very reasonable fees, and what we hear from clients, more often than not, is, "Best money I ever spent."

I don't say this as a plug, but rather to let you know that hundreds of business owners have told us specifically that this is one of the SEO-related programs that really make a difference with regard to obtaining increased local credibility.

Pay Per Click Advertising

Challenge:

Gaining a local advantage in PPC can be tricky but is well worth the effort. This is where the lines between territories tend to become fine, as most search engine PPC programs work based on selecting a radius in miles rather than by zip codes.

We touched on this somewhat when discussing radius of PPC search, but now we will dig in deeper and really boost your ROI. After all, the purpose of this book is to increase your profit through improved online marketing presence.

Step by Step Solution: PPC

Step 1: As mentioned before, a list of eligible keywords is defined by Corporate. And again, this is with the understanding that the approved "GEO" name (city, town, state, etc.) can be added before or after the keyword by the franchisee - if they so wish.

Step 2: The franchisor develops a list of "city limits" the franchisee can advertise in, without poaching another franchisee's territory. This list is made public to all franchisees for evaluation so there will be no future misunderstandings.

Step 3: The franchisee plots out a maximum allowable advertising radius, based on the aforementioned city limits. This list is compared against the zip code map (to be compared to your radius map) for approval by the franchisor.

Step 4: Standardized PPC ads, for each keyword in the approved list, are developed by Corporate and banked for access and use by franchisees. Again, these can be modified with the GEO name by the franchisee if previously agreed.

Note: *It is also often VERY beneficial to use common GEO names as we discussed in Section One "Controlling the Message". These might be "East End", "West End", "Northside", "Southside", "Bayside" or more specific locations like "Southie" for South Boston, MA or "The Village" for Greenwich Village in New York City.*

The value comes from familiarity and a sense of local flavor. Do NOT underestimate this - especially in PPC where the cost and position of your ads are greatly determined by Quality Score, which will be higher if more people like your ad and trust it.

Step 5: Several possible PPC landing pages are developed and made accessible to franchisees, each with a slant toward GEO targeting (unlike in "Controlling the Message", where we wanted more variety).

Step 6: The local PPC ad is crafted to take advantage of any local considerations, such as phone number, city or town name, etc.

Windshields from $99.00
www.WindshieldInstall.com
Affordable Windshield/Auto Glass
installed in Short Pump. Call today!

We looked at this same example a while ago so you already know what was changed from the original, but we also changed one more thing: "Richmond" to "Short Pump". This is because Short Pump is a section of Richmond, Virginia that has started getting a lot of local search over the past year or so. This is just a minor tweak to help increase ROI.

Putting It All Together: PPC

If local PPC is an option, we have found it is well worth the effort and the additional processes - for both the franchisee and franchisor. Just be sure to follow the steps laid out here carefully as that will help improve quality score, which in turn will decrease cost-per-click spend and possibly increase placement.

Social Media

Challenge:

The challenge in Social Media doesn't really go beyond that discussed in Section One; "Controlling the Message" and Section Two; "Branding/Marketing Flexibility".

I won't repeat all of that here because it's more than just a few paragraphs like other snippets, repeated merely for your quick convenience.

Instead let's use our time to focus on something new that we can start using right away...

Part Five: Getting New Business

What We All Want:

Last time, I promise - A final reminder of what everyone wants in order to succeed; this time with regard to getting new business.

Franchisors want...

✓ to market to both consumers and potential franchisees

In comparison, franchisees want...

✓ to beat the local competition and maximize profit

This is really what it's all about. Web design is important but it does not guarantee new business. The same can be said for SEO. But again, mine is a method of Conversion Based

SEO, which encompasses elements of web design to maximize effect. Throughout this short book we have looked at ways to tackle individual challenges such as controlling the message, protecting the brand, having marketing flexibility, managing the web presence and showing up in the geographical areas that matter most. This has all led up to the ultimate goal of getting new business.

Of all challenges thus far, this is the easiest - and briefest - to summarize in perspectives.

Franchisor:

"I need to get new franchisees while taking care of the current ones."

Franchisee:

"I need to get new business so I can stay in business - but more, I want to make a greater profit so I can retire someday."

Experience:

It's been my experience that both goals are very realistic and very attainable. In fact, that's an understatement. Getting you more business, and increasing profits, is the very reason NetSearch Direct exists.

This is unlike any other section so far in that it's less about how to get the visitors to your site and more about how to turn those visitors into leads or sales once they are there. So let's take this final step into how we can make this happen.

Three Keys to Conversions

There are three primary keys to conversion. These can be broken down even further into dozens - or even hundreds - but it all comes back to these three:

1. The Call to Action (CTA)
2. The Offer
3. Asking For the Sale

Let's explore them one by one and then look at some general, and more specific, examples of how we can best implement each...

First Key - The Call to Action (CTA)

Think of the call to action (CTA) as the "lead maker". This is where you get the passive visitor to become an active participant by doing something (usually requesting information or to be contacted). Typical vehicles for a CTA are online form fills, phone calls and emails. We will review each along with some tips to get the best return for your efforts.

Form Fill: A great way to get all the information you need from someone, at their convenience, is with a simple form fill. Note that I said "simple". As a rule of thumb, for every field of required information you request, you will lose about 10% of the audience. That said, if you can have a nice short form ('name', 'best phone number OR email to reach you', and a box for 'optional comments or questions') you will get the most form fills.

We have found that from 34% to 37% of website visitors prefer this method - depending on the industry and what will best meet their needs.

Here are a few more ways to ensure you receive maximum form fills:

➢ Place a short contact form on each page of your site, not just the "Contact Us" page.

➢ Put the form in the same place on each page, keeping it as consistent as you are able.

➢ Always have a "Thank You" page appear after the "Submit" button has been clicked on the form. The thank you page should tell the user their request has been submitted, provide a thank you message for taking the time to contact you, and a note stating, "If you have any additional questions or need immediate assistance during our business hours (and show them), please feel free to call us at xxx-xxx-xxxx."

➢ Make sure the "Thank You" page has a unique, 'thank you' or 'message sent' URL such as "main-site.com/thank-you.html" so you can track form fills via analytics software as well as by email receipt of that form. This is VERY important.

➢ Do NOT use a captcha code if you can avoid it. They might help reduce spam but most people hate them - especially the really complex ones (warped text, colored dots in the background, etc.)

➢ If you must use a captcha, make it a simple one. Use either real words or easy math problems such as $3 + 1 = ?$

➢ Phone Number: In our experience, about 56% to 60% of visitors would rather pick up the phone than fill out a form. Of course, this depends on the industry and their goal, but 56% is a good typical number to consider as a jumping off point.

Here are a few tips to help get as many phone calls as possible:

➢ Place your phone number at the top of the page - on every page, in the same spot. We have found the upper-right portion of the masthead to be the optimal spot, with top-center being the second.

➢ Make sure the numbers are big and easy to see. This means you should use a heavily contrasting color (compared to the page background) in an easy-to-read font like Arial, in a point-size two to three times the size of your page text. And, of course, bolding the text is usually optimal.

➢ Make sure the phone number is displayed as text rather than as part of an image. With the proper java scripts running on the site, text phone numbers allow you to track calls so you can know exactly what leads came in from SEO, versus PPC, versus those who simply typed in your URL or followed a Social link. This is known as "call tracking" and is VERY worthwhile.

➢ Try to place your phone number within the verbiage of your page.

Here's a quiz... Do you know why marketers have been placing "Call Now!" in their ads for over forty years? Because it works.

"Do you know why marketers have been placing "Call Now!" in their ads for the past fifty years? Because it works."

Email: Email was once the premier way for people to contact a site administrator or request more information, but email harvesting software that is responsible for billions of spam messages per day has changed all that. Now it accounts for less than 10% of our client's site contact, on average.

It's still a good idea to include an email contact address - but only if you actually want to receive email. If you do not check it regularly, having this contact option can backfire terribly. A lot of people believe that email, because it offers instant delivery, should garner quick response. Not everyone of course, but do you really want to upset a potential customer before they even have a chance to get to know you?

If you opt to include email contact info on your site, here are a few tips to help get the most out of it:

➢ To maximize leads and minimize spam, make your address easy but not obvious. Every spammer in the world knows that "admin@" or "sales@" and "contact@" will work as genuine email addresses for just about any commercial domain name. Why do I mention spam? Because if you get too much of it, you are very likely to miss genuine leads. And the only thing worse than not getting a lead is getting one and ignoring it, because of the damage that can do to your reputation. Nobody likes to be ignored - especially prospective customers.

➢ Place your email address at the top of the page, directly opposite the phone number.

➢ Unlike the phone number, make your email address a clickable image rather than text. This will stop most email address harvesting apps from getting it. Of course, if you make the image clickable, with the actual address as the destination in the HTML code, some software will still be able to get it. Still, risking spam is better than asking a person to retype your address.

Second Key - The Offer

When it comes to sales, without a strong offer you might as well just say, "We want your business, I guess."

Although a strong offer can benefit any aspect of online marketing, it affects us most greatly in PPC. This is because you have driven your visitor (AKA prospect) to a specific landing page containing the offer. You have a bit more latitude in SEO - although you should certainly have a strong offer on any sales pages.

The advice I suggest for maximizing the effectiveness of the offer is very simple, and you have probably heard it many times before in other aspects of sales:

Perception is everything. Provide an offer that has the highest perceived value available.

It might be a discount or a free bonus that actually costs you very little, or maybe free shipping. What matters is how valuable it is perceived to be.

Case in point: I had the opportunity to work with a woman who had answered the phones for a number of well-known infomercials and she observed that most people began their transaction by ensuring they had qualified for the "free bonus" or "free shipping". It seems they cared more for the throw-in than for the product they were buying - at least at that particular moment. Unusual? Is it? Don't you find that you like getting the best deal possible - and that you feel like you "won" each time you do? That's the real power of a strong offer.

Forget logic; trigger emotion. No matter what we, as intelligent beings, like to believe - the truth is we make purchases based on emotional decisions rather than logical. Give your offer strong emotional ties and you will be amazed at how sales increase. People have choices in where they buy, so make them feel great about their decision to do business with you.

Features take a back seat to benefits. I can best describe this with an example I experienced firsthand. This past January, my wife decided she wanted a new winter coat. At her favorite department store, a salesperson approached her and recommended a coat "made from the finest fleece" that was "hand stitched". She thanked the salesperson and said, "I don't think that's what I want". Thirty minutes and two laps around the department later, a second salesperson came up and said, "Oh! You'd look great in this coat! It's so warm and so very comfortable." My wife promptly tried it on, proudly modeled it for me, and bought it - thanking the salesperson profusely for the help.

It was the same coat the first salesperson had shown her - just on a different rack and with a different presentation (one of benefits and an emotional tie rather than features). When I pointed to the original coat upon leaving, she took hers out of its long white garment bag and said, "Hmm... I guess it is. But this one just sounded so much nicer."

Notice what she said? The exact same coat "sounded nicer". That speaks volumes because that logic works for every single person I have ever met - myself included.

Third Key - Asking For the Sale

Believe it or not, the most common issue I see with regard to otherwise great marketing tactics is that most people very seldom ask for the sale. Oh sure, they hint at it and provide ways people can buy - but they almost never come right out and ask for the sale.

Repeat after me... "Buy my product and you will be glad you did." And mean it! If your product is the best, you are doing a great service to anyone who buys it. Don't ever forget that.

"Repeat after me... Buy my product and you will be glad you did."

At this time, NetSearch Direct has 600 clients spanning North America; more than a quarter of which are franchises. Of those, 75% have been with us for well over a year. This is because those who invested in our services were glad they did.

Get a Free Site Snapshot!

NetSearchDirect.com   Fax to: 804.228.4479

Name:_____

Company:_____

Email:_____

Phone:_____ **Fax:**_____

Please complete this info and fax it to 804.228.4479 (or you can email the info to mikem@netsearchdirect.com). Once received we can have a **Free Search Engine Snapshot Report** back to you within a few days, then answer any questions you might have.

Web Address:

*http://www.*_____

Keywords (What words or 'search terms' do you want to be found for?)

_____

_____

_____

GEOs (What state and cities do you want to be found for?) *i.e. "Richmond, VA"*

_____

_____

_____

That's it. Please fax to 804.228.4479. We'll be in touch soon. Thanks!

Glossary

7-Pack - The group of seven local business listings that Google provides at the top of the search engine results page for certain types of searches.

Ad position - In the world of PPC, ad position is really just where your ad is shown on the web page. Top placements are typically more expensive, and for good reason – they get more clicks. But position is based on more than money. Your ad has to have a good quality score as well.

AdWords - Google's AdWords is a "pay for placement" text advertising program. You can display your ads on Google and you only pay if people click on them (cost per click) – or by the number of impressions shown (CPM) – as you choose.

You can create ads and use keywords based on your business to attract more customers through searches on Google or any relevant resource you like in the AdSense network. It's simple. People search for an item or service by using a keyword. If you bid on that keyword (and bid high enough) your ad is shown and you either pay per click or by the number of impressions. Although PPC is the most common method advertisers choose, Google has been known to experiment with alternative methods such as "cost per action" (CPA) that has the advertiser paying only when a call to action has been completed.

Algorithm - Math guys will probably have a more accurate definition of this term, but in the search engine world, algorithm refers to the complex formula search engines use to determine which websites to display, and in what order, on a search engine results page. Algorithms are frequently tweaked by the search engines to try and provide results that most closely match a searcher's intention.

Bidding (or Keyword Bidding) - No big surprise here. Bidding means placing a bid price that you are willing to pay as an advertiser on a pay-per-click search engine. The highest bid for a given keyword achieves the top spot in the PPC search results – with some exceptions.

Google throws "a monkey in the wrench" with its whole "ad quality score" deal, where you bid to be in a group (say, the top three places) and a complex method to determine your actual placement is used, such as ad relevance to the target URL page, wording of the ad, and popularity of the ad based on click through rate.

In other words, you might pay more to be number three than the person who is showing up as number one. It all depends on your quality score.

Black Hat SEO - Any optimization tactic that causes a site to rank more highly than its content would otherwise justify – until it gets busted. As the name indicates, these techniques are considered unwelcome by the major search engines. However, they are still used today, more than ever, due to the lure of easy rankings and ease of starting over if busted. Be warned however, it's not that easy. Some search engines, like Google, will do their best to make it extremely difficult for offenders to ever rank again in their network, and, if you make the blacklist, any search network.

Blacklist - A blacklist is literally a list of those websites banned by search engines, for whatever reason. Most major search engines compile their own lists, consisting mostly of spammers and those who use other black hat tricks. But, there's more. These lists get shared across search networks and it's not just a list of websites anymore. Now the list can include IP addresses and even personal information about the site owner. Having your site blacklisted = bad, so choosing a reputable and ethical SEO provider is very desirable.

Bot - Bot is short for robot. Also known as "spiders" and "crawlers", they are programs used by a search engine to explore the web by following all available links. They do not work alone, however. Once a bot has found a page to scan, it works with an indexer to download the HTML content and store it in a database that returns the search listings.

Broad Match - Broad Match is a form of "keyword matching" used in pay-per-click advertising campaigns. It refers to the matching of a search listing or advertisement to selected keywords in any order. Broad match terms are less targeted than "exact" or "phrase" matches.

For example, if a person searches for "Michelin brand tires" and your ad campaign is set to "broad match", your ad is eligible to be shown for "Michelin" or "tires" or "brand tires," etc. – in addition to the full search term of "Michelin brand tires."

Call to Action (CTA) - A call to action is any method used in advertising to encourage a person to complete a task as defined by the advertiser. It is usually a combination of text and graphics that encourage the user to complete a form, click a link, or even pick up the phone and make a call. You see them all the time with words like "Click here," "Buy now," "Enter now," or "Click to download."

Captcha - You've surely run across those boxes with often undecipherable words and combinations of letters that – ironically –

you're required to decipher in order to submit a form on a web page. Those are captchas, and their purpose is to make sure there's a human at the keyboard, rather than a bot written by some clever programmer to send the site owner 37,000 emails for discount prescriptions.

Clickthrough - A clickthrough is the action of clicking on a link and causing a redirect to another web page. It is basically the act of clicking "through" a link to get to the "offer" or "end result" page.

Clickthrough rate (CTR) - As with all things associated with advertising, if it's not measurable, it's not meaningful. An ad's clickthrough rate is basically its success rate. This is determined by a simple formula of dividing the number of clicks on an ad by the number of times that ad was shown (the number of impressions).

Conversion - A conversion in online terms is basically the same as in traditional offline terms. The act of transforming a website visitor into a customer is "customer conversion", while the act of taking that visitor a step closer to becoming a paying customer can be considered a "lead conversion".

Conversion rate - Conversion rate, much like clickthrough rate, is the rate at which visitors to a site get converted to customers or leads. The lead conversion rate is calculated by dividing the number of visitors who completed a goal (that is, made a phone call, filled out a web form, or sent an email) by the total number of visitors. The ability to calculate things like this separates SEO and PPC from more traditional forms of advertising by making it easier to measure a campaign's effectiveness.

Cost Per Action (CPA) - Cost per action is the expense incurred or price paid for a specific action, such as signing up for an email newsletter. If you pay $1 per click and it takes 20 clicks to get a visitor to complete an action, then the CPA is $20.

Cost Per Click (CPC) - This is the price paid for a clickthrough of your ad in PPC.

Cost Per Lead (CPL) - Cost per lead is simply the average price paid to attain a new lead. Its formula is very simple. Just take the amount spent and divide it by the number of leads generated. If you get 20 leads from a campaign that costs $100, your cost per lead is $5.

Cost Per Order (CPO) - Cost per order is just like CPL; just replace "lead" with "order." If you get 50 orders from an advertising campaign that costs $500, your CPO is $10. Note: CPO is also known as cost-per-transaction, or CPT.

Cost Per Sale (CPS) - CPS is a representation of the sales revenue divided by total ad spend, with that number divided by the number of units sold.

Cost Per Thousand (CPM) - CPM is the price paid for one thousand impressions of an advertising campaign. It is a bit confusing because the "M" in CPM is a holdover from earlier marketing days when the "M" was used as a sort of shorthand for the Roman numeral "M", which is the number one thousand.

Crawler - A crawler is just another name for a "spider" or "bot", which are programs used by a search engine to explore the web by following all available links. They do not work alone, however. Once a crawler has found a page to scan it works with an indexer to download the HTML content and store it in a database that returns the search listings.

Directory - A directory is similar to a search engine in that it provides results for items searched on the web. It differs however in that in a directory, human editors group websites into categories and provide site descriptions or edit descriptions that are submitted to them. In a search engine, this is all handled by bots and indexing software that run constantly. Yahoo! was the original directory and continued to post directory results until the mid 2000's.

Exact Match - Exact match is a form of keyword matching where the search query must be exactly the same as the advertisement keyword. Let's use our Michelin example again...

If a person searches for "Michelin brand tires" and your ad campaign is set to "exact match", your ad is NOT eligible to be shown for just the terms "Michelin," or "tires," or even "brand tires." It is ONLY eligible to be shown for the full and exact search term of "Michelin brand tires."

This gives the advertiser an opportunity to be extremely precise in deciding what he or she is willing to pay for.

Exact Match Domain - An exact match domain is when the domain name exactly matches the keyword searched in a search engine or directory. This can be very powerful in terms of SEO advantage if the SEO person knows what they are doing.

Geo-Targeting - Geo-targeting is a method of very targeted advertising in which ads are distributed based on geographic location. Online advertising, like Google AdWords, allows for the geo-targeting of countries, states, cities, and suburbs. You can also geo-target in SEO. This is when you optimize for a keyword that includes the geographic qualifier (IE/ city name) as part of the keyword. For example: "New York City pizza delivery."

Google - Google is currently the world's number one search engine with the lion's share of the word's search engine market share (typically between 50% and 60%). Nipping at its heels, constantly striving to get a bigger piece of the pie, are Yahoo! and Bing.

Fun Fact: Founders Larry Page and Sergey Brin named the search engine they built "Google" as a play on the word "googol" the mathematical term for a 1 followed by 100 zeros.

Just for fun, here is a googol:

10,000,000,000,000,000,000,000,000,000,0
00,000,000,000,000,000,000,000,000,000,0
00,000,000,000,000,000,000,000,000,000,0
00

The name reflects the immense volume of information that exists, and the scope of Google's mission: "to organize the world's information and make it universally accessible and useful."

Google AdSense - AdSense is a free advertising revenue share program that lets online publishers earn money by displaying relevant ads on their websites (and other online media). Here's how it works:

You, as the AdSense affiliate, place an ad block on your site. The ad block shows paid text ads that are relevant to your visitor by being relevant to your page content.

When someone clicks on the ads you placed on your site, you earn revenue. This is typically a cost-per-click revenue model, wherein you get paid X amount for every click – although you usually never know the exact value of X until after you earn the money.

Google Analytics - This is a free web analytics tool, requiring nothing more than a small bit of JavaScript code on your pages, that offers a great deal of detailed visitor statistics. Google Analytics can be used to track all the usual site activities: visits, page views, pages viewed per visit, bounce rate, average time on site, and much more.

Google Traffic Estimator - Google Traffic Estimator is a tool that indicates the number of clicks to expect on Google AdWords ads for particular keywords. It is used to help the advertiser estimate search volume, average CPC, likely ad position, estimated clicks per day and cost per day.

Hosting environment - This is the place where all of the data, photos, text, etc. that make up your website actually lives. That is, every website has an actual, physical server that holds the information that makes the individual web pages. Any number of companies offer hosting services, with any number of pricing plans. The idea is to ensure quality and dependability of service from whatever provider you choose.

HTML - Hyper Text Markup Language. The primary language of the internet, HTML is the code behind web pages.

Impression - An impression is one "serving" of a search advertisement to one user session.

Keyword - A keyword (officially called a query in tech terms) is a word (or group of words) that a search engine user uses to find relevant web pages.

Keyword Density - Keyword density is the number of occurrences that a given keyword appears on a web page. The more times that a given word appears on your page the more weight that word is assigned by the search engine.

Keyword Efficiency - Keyword efficiency is a measure of how effective a keyword will be when used in an SEO campaign. This is such a big deal that there are a number of specialized formulas out there to help determine that efficiency, such as…

Keyword Efficiency Index - The Keyword efficiency index is a factor generated by using a KEI formula that takes into account the search volume and the number of competing web pages. It's used to measure the potential SEO impact of individual keywords. But don't read too deeply into that. It is not a magic bullet to tell you what keywords will be easiest to rank for. Think of it more as "bang for your buck" indicator with many variations.

Keyword Efficiency Index with Relevancy - Keyword efficiency index with relevancy (KEI R) is the same as the keyword efficiency index formula, only it includes the relevance factor of your keyword that you manually insert, to help determine its most accurate value.

Keyword Matching - Keyword matching is the process of selecting and providing advertising or information that match the user's search query. There are four types of keyword matching: broad match, exact match, phrase match, and negative keyword.

Keyword Phrase - A keyword phrase is a search phrase made up of any number of keywords. Most people use "keyword" and "keyword phrase" interchangeably because it is not often today that people optimize for a single "one-word" keyword.

Keyword Popularity - Just like it sounds, keyword popularity is a term used to describe how in-demand any given keyword is, at any given time – based on how many people are searching for it (search volume).

Keyword Prominence - This indicates the location of a given keyword on the web page. The higher up in the page (or closer to the beginning of the spiderable portion of the page) a particular word is, the more prominence it has. The more prominent the keyword, the more value that particular term is assigned by the search engine when it matches a keyword search.

Keyword Research - Keyword research is the due-diligence performed to determine the words and phrases that people use to find something online. Once determined, the keywords are compiled into a list for use in the SEO efforts.

Keyword Stuffing - Keyword stuffing is placing an excessive number of keywords into a web page. It typically refers to having too many instances of one or more keywords rather than too many separate keywords.

Keyword-rich - Keyword-rich refers to when a web page or chunk of text is full of good keywords rather than a bunch of meaningless words or irrelevant words. Taking it a step further, it also means that each keyword is used an appropriate number of times compared to the amount of overall content. Note: This is important!

Landing Page - A landing page is a web page where people go to once they click on an online advertisement or natural search listing. Landing pages are carefully designed to be extremely relevant to the advertisement or search listing. Of course, it's easy to build a highly relevant landing page because you can design it to target just a single (or multiple) specific keyword(s) or theme(s).

Link Building - Link building is actively researching, finding, and obtaining links from websites for the purpose of increasing your "link popularity" and/or Google "PageRank" – and ultimately, ranking.

Meta Description - Meta "description" is a tag in the HTML that describes the page's content. This is not visible on the actual web page but is very visible as the description in the search results – so make it good.

Meta Keywords - Meta "keywords" is a tag in the HTML that lists keywords relevant to the page's content. Tip: Use only keywords that are visible on the page, otherwise it looks like spamming to the search engine.

Meta Tags - A Meta tag is information that is associated with a web page and placed in the HTML but not visible on the displayed web page.

Organic results - These are the non-paid-for results that a search engine such as Google, Yahoo, or Bing provides from a query.

Organic (SEO) results are often just below the paid results and typically more highly regarded by people who are searching.

Pay-Per-Click (PPC) - This is paid-for advertising on search engine results pages (as well as sponsored sites), usually at the top and/or side of the organic results. PPC is based on an automated auction system, where the cost of an ad depends on the popularity of the keywords for the ad and the position of the ad on the page. As the name implies, charges only apply if an ad is actually clicked. PPC offers immediate results, unlike SEO which may take some time to manifest.

Page Title - A page title simply what you call the page, inserted into the Title tag. It is also one of the more urgent parts of onsite optimization to get right.

PageRank (PR) - There's no way I can improve on this so I'll let Wikipedia explain this one...

"PageRank is a link analysis algorithm, named after Larry Page, used by the Google Internet search engine that assigns a numerical weighting to each element of a hyperlinked set of documents, such as the World Wide Web, with the purpose of "measuring" its relative importance within the set. The algorithm may be applied to any collection of entities with reciprocal quotations and references. The numerical weight that it assigns to any given element E is referred to as the PageRank of E and denoted by PR(E).

The name "PageRank" is a trademark of Google, and the PageRank process has been patented (U.S. Patent 6,285,999). However, the patent is assigned to Stanford University and not to Google. Google has exclusive license rights on the patent from Stanford University. The university received 1.8 million shares of Google in exchange for use of the patent; the shares *were sold in 2005 for $336 million." – Wikipedia.org*

Reference:
http://en.wikipedia.org/wiki/PageRank

Phrase Match - Phrase Match is a form of keyword matching where an ad will be displayed if the user's search includes the exact phrase, even if their search contains additional words.

QR code - Short for Quick Response code. This is in essence an updated version of the barcode. It looks something like a black and white version of a really low resolution video game explosion, in a square, on the corners of signs and packages, in print advertising, and just about everywhere. Smart phones typically have QR code readers that will allow the user to scan the code rather than typing in a website for more information about a product.

Quality score - Search engines (Google, in particular) use algorithms to calculate the value of a PPC ad you've created in relation to the keywords you want to target with that ad. It takes into account things like the relevance of the keyword to the ad, the relevance of the keyword and the ad to the actual search, the quality of the destination link (your landing page or website), and many more. If you choose to target the keyword "cat slippers" but your ad content is touting a new water-melon-and-wheat-bran weight loss solution, you're going to have a low quality score. Unless it targets weight loss for cats wearing slippers.

Query - A query is another term for a search. When used as a verb, it is basically performing a keyword based search in a search engine. When used as a noun, it refers to the actual keyword phrase the searcher types in to the search engine. To keep it simple, you can just think of a query as a keyword or the act of entering a keyword into a search engine.

ROI - Return On Investment. The benefit gained in return for the cost of investing into advertising for a project, such as an SEO campaign. It can be measured easily as: "total revenues (generated from campaign or project) minus total costs."

RSS feed - This is a method for getting web content that changes regularly in a standard format, without having to visit the site. For example, if you have a favorite blog that offers RSS Feeds, you can have each update sent to your RSS aggregator (Microsoft Outlook supports this, and the feeds have the appearance of emails).

Search Engine Marketing (SEM) - SEM, or search engine marketing, is basically any online advertising or publicity method that harnesses the power of search engines as the advertising medium. It includes, but is certainly not limited to, search engine optimization (SEO), pay-per-click (PPC), paid space placement, and contextual advertising.

Search Engine Optimization (SEO) - Not optimizing search engines, but rather, optimizing your website so that is friendly to search engines. Proper SEO results in higher visibility in search results when someone searches for the products, goods, or services your company provides.

SERP - Search Engine Results Page. That's the list of results you get when you type in "find a dog house architect" (or some other search term) into your search engine of choice. From a business perspective, it probably goes without saying that being near the top of that list is preferable. The number of searchers who click a link on the list diminishes greatly as you travel down the page, and even more so on subsequent SERPs (page 347 is not where you want to be).

Social media - Social media encompasses a wide variety of sites and services on the internet, with the common thread that each has a broad base of users who share information. Facebook is the big player, followed by Twitter, Google+, LinkedIn, and others. With users in the hundreds of millions – both individuals and businesses – social media provides almost unequaled opportunities for businesses to be seen.

Text Ad - A text ad is (typically) action oriented copy describing the product or service that is being advertised. The text ad appears alongside natural search results (but looks different from organic listings and is labeled as "sponsored") and links to a specified web page.

Theme - A theme can be most easily defined as the main keyword focus of a web page. The theme of a website relates to what the whole site is about or the kind of information the content is relaying.

Traffic - Traffic refers to the users (and number of) that visit a website.

Tweet - A posting on Twitter. Tweets are limited to 140 characters, so you have to be concise. Using a hashtag (#) in front of a word in your tweet serves to place it in a category so it can be found by other Twitter users searching for posts on that subject. You can also retweet a message someone else has posted, which is one of the most powerful features of this service – the potential for exponential message distribution.

Unique Visitors - Unique visitors are a count of individual users who have accessed your web site. This is different from "hits," as hits count multiple visits from the same user.

User Generated Content - User generated content is content created and published by a variety of end users online. Types of user generated content are wide and varied and may include videos, podcasts and posts on discussion groups, blogs, wikis, and social media sites.

URL - Uniform Resource Locator. That helps, doesn't it? I thought not. A URL is basically the web address of a site, like www.netsearchdirect.com. For SEO purposes, the closer you can get the URL to a keyword theme you'd like to focus on, the better. If you sell sardine-flavored ginger snap cookies, www.sardinegingersnaps.com or, possibly even www.sardinecookies.com are excellent choices.

Viral - A term coined to describe sudden and exponential popularity for something shared in social media. Viral videos or tweets (Twitter messages) can generate millions of views and/or shares in a matter of days.

Visibility - Visibility is how well-placed or how visible your website is in the search engines for relevant keyword searches. It generally refers to being well-ranked and easily found when people are searching for the products or services you offer.

Yahoo! - Yahoo is the original friendly Internet search system. Until the early 2000's it served solely as a directory (a collection of Internet sites organized by subject, entered by site managers, then reviewed by human editors) rather than a true search engine, which send out a spider to crawl as many documents as possible and an indexer that reads each page or document and generates an index based on the information within each document.

Today, it has both a search engine and directory, with the search engine serving up the default SERPs (search engine results page). And, although it costs $299 to apply for listing in the directory, it is a wise investment for serious online businesses as it will add credibility to your site from any search engine's perspective.

Note: *In late August 2010, Yahoo! began showing Bing's search results. Yahoo! is still Yahoo! but the results are Bing's – although actual placement on the page can vary (stay tuned for how this shakes out.)*

Some History: Originally created in 1994, by Jerry Yang and David Filo, as a way to keep track of interesting links on the Internet, Yahoo was first called "Jerry and David's Guide to the World Wide Web."

They ran it from their personal computers at Stanford University while completing their PhD's in electrical engineering. Of course that name was a bit long so they came up with an acronym that had a double meaning - Yahoo! is short for "Yet Another Hierarchical Officious Oracle," which happens to be a word they liked the general definition of; yahoo: "rude, unsophisticated, or uncouth."

Index

213

215

216

About the Author

In 1982 when Mike began his career in advertising, he was moved by these words from Zig Ziglar, a legendary salesman and sales trainer: "You will get all you want out of life if you help enough other people get what they want." Nearly thirty years later these words still ring true. For Mike it's a good day when he has helped someone else be successful - and he has a lot of good days.

With over a quarter century in direct marketing, success has come to Mike in several ways. He is the CEO and President of Marketing Partners. Inc., one of the Southeast's largest direct marketing firms. In 2006, he built on this direct-marketing success by founding NetSearch Direct; a Search Engine Optimization and Marketing/Social Media company headquartered in Richmond Virginia.

From a small shop with a handful of specialists NetSearch Direct managed to double in size during the worst economy in 30 years. As of this writing (August 2014), we have quadrupled in size. Thanks to some great successes, lucky breaks and plenty of hard work NSD now provides profit-producing results to approximately six hundred businesses throughout the United States.

Mike is the proud father of two young-adult daughters and firmly believes that whatever success has come his way has been primarily because of hard work, luck, more hard work and luck, and support from his wife of twenty-seven years, Helene.

Mike can be reached at 804-228-4400 or via email at: mikem@netsearchdirect.com.

Free Snapshot Report Form

NetSearchDirect.com   Fax to: 804.228.4479

Name: _____

Company:_____

Email:_____

Phone: _____   Fax:_____

Please complete this info and fax it to 804.228.4479 (or you can email the info to mikem@netsearchdirect.com). Once received we can have a Free Search Engine Snapshot Report back to you within a few days, then answer any questions you might have.

Web Address:

*http://www.*_____

Keywords (What words or 'search terms' do you want to be found for?)

_____

_____

_____

GEOs (What state and cities do you want to be found for?) i.e. "Richmond, VA"

_____

_____

_____

That's it. Please fax to 804.228.4479. We'll be in touch soon. Thanks!

Made in the USA
San Bernardino, CA
25 August 2014